MAKING IT

1968 POEMS

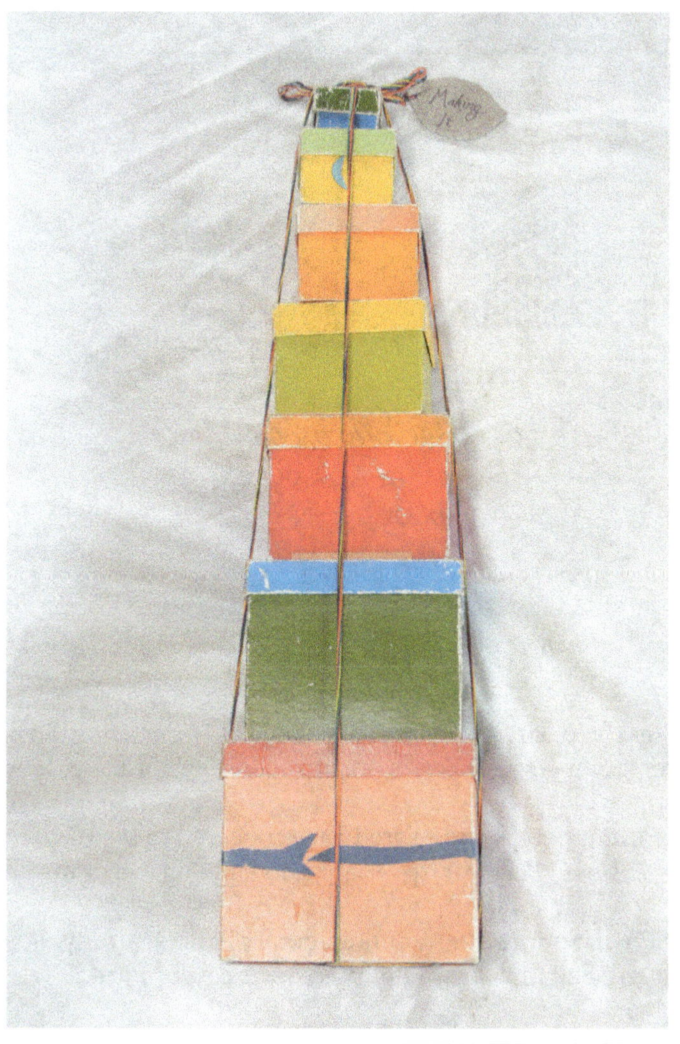

the book & the events

larry goodell
2023

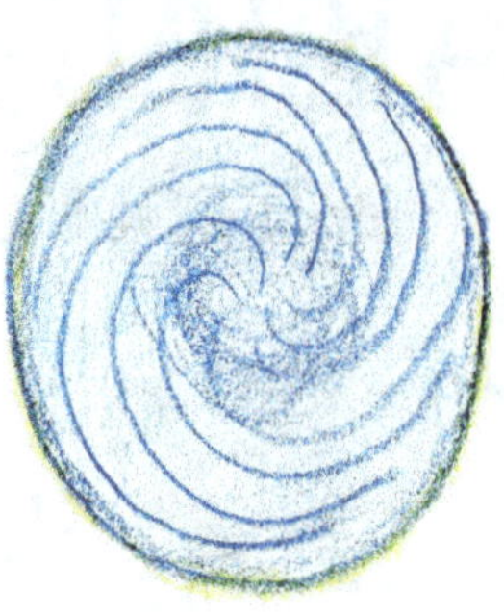

an offshoot of space

rediscovering delight

there is a blue
there is a blue
plate
in the window

light shines thru

"Bag for the 6 Directions" was presented at "Concentration 85-86" Contemporary Music Series organized by Dwight Loop, March 1986.

Some event poems and related have appeared in the blog *3 Dimensional Poetry* https://larrygoodell.blogspot.com/

ARTSPACE Southwestern Contemporary Arts Quarterly, Volume 1, Number 1, Fall 1976, first published my excerpt pp 131-2.

DUENDE PRESS *the original*
po box 571 placitas, new mexico 87043

THE BOOK - POEMS from 1968

Here are the reproduced pages of this '68 assembled poetry "book" reproduced best I can. It is a one-only-book I made from work that year, and it was in a box attacked by bookworms. I cut out insect damage of page edges that were on the bottom of the box where the worst harm was, and repaired pages by extending them out to where their edge should be. In doing this I found I greatly valued this 1968 creative work. The original is 3 hole letter size bound with leather thongs.

I'm including the EVENT POEMS from 1968 so that all my work from that year can be seen together. *lg*

Note:
Lines to the right of margin in poems
are correspondingly read at slightly higher pitch.

Clarifications I have added are in italics.

Repaired edges of some pages.

CONTENTS OF MAKING IT

from 1968 - larry goodell

1968

Larry Goodell

FOCAL POINT
UNSPOKEN
GOD IS A TURBAGE FACTORY

/Jan

THE GREEN THIEF
MIDI
SONG OF THE EXTERIOR FOLD
CANIPTIONS IN FIT METER
A SET OF 4 cymbalation for Tosh – late Feb
/Feb

SONG FOR SPRING
THE FEAST OF DREAMS
THE LIGHT THAT IS FOREVER IN OUR DREAMS
/Mar

TIME IN FAILING ORDER
EVOLUTION A TROIS
4 POEMS
A PEA
THE CIRCUMSCRIBED GENERATION

MAN HOODED
AN OFFSHOOT OF SPACE
/Apr

THE IRIS LEAVES
OFF-CENTER
MAKING IT
ENTRANCE
JEWEL
THE FOOL
/May

*green show where chapters of A NEW LAND go
*grey indicate a doings (event-poem)

SPACE ORB VISION CROWN
THE FOOL
DISCORD
THE AMERICAN PARTY
THE FOOL
FOR OLIVIA'S BIRTHDAY
3 POEMS AROUND A BIRTHDAY
SONG
CORRIDOR OUT
CIRCLE DANCE /CLARITY IS THE BREATH OF ANGEL
THE GOD (or) SHUFFLE
/Jun

SCULPTOR OF THE CALENDAR STONE
LEAF FROM A FALLING TREE
/Jul

HITLER
MUDHEAD SONG
/Aug

A SET OF LOOK-THRUS FOR 3-DIMENSIONAL VISION
DEAR GOD
WORD MANDALA
/Sep

THE POWERS WORK THRU A MOVING FOCUS
THE COUPLE
SING IN POSSESSION OF YR SOUL
WAR GAME
BUT IS (not here)
/Oct

LIFESAVER
THE PRESIDENT
/Nov

SHE'S BEEN THERE ALL THE TIME
/Dec

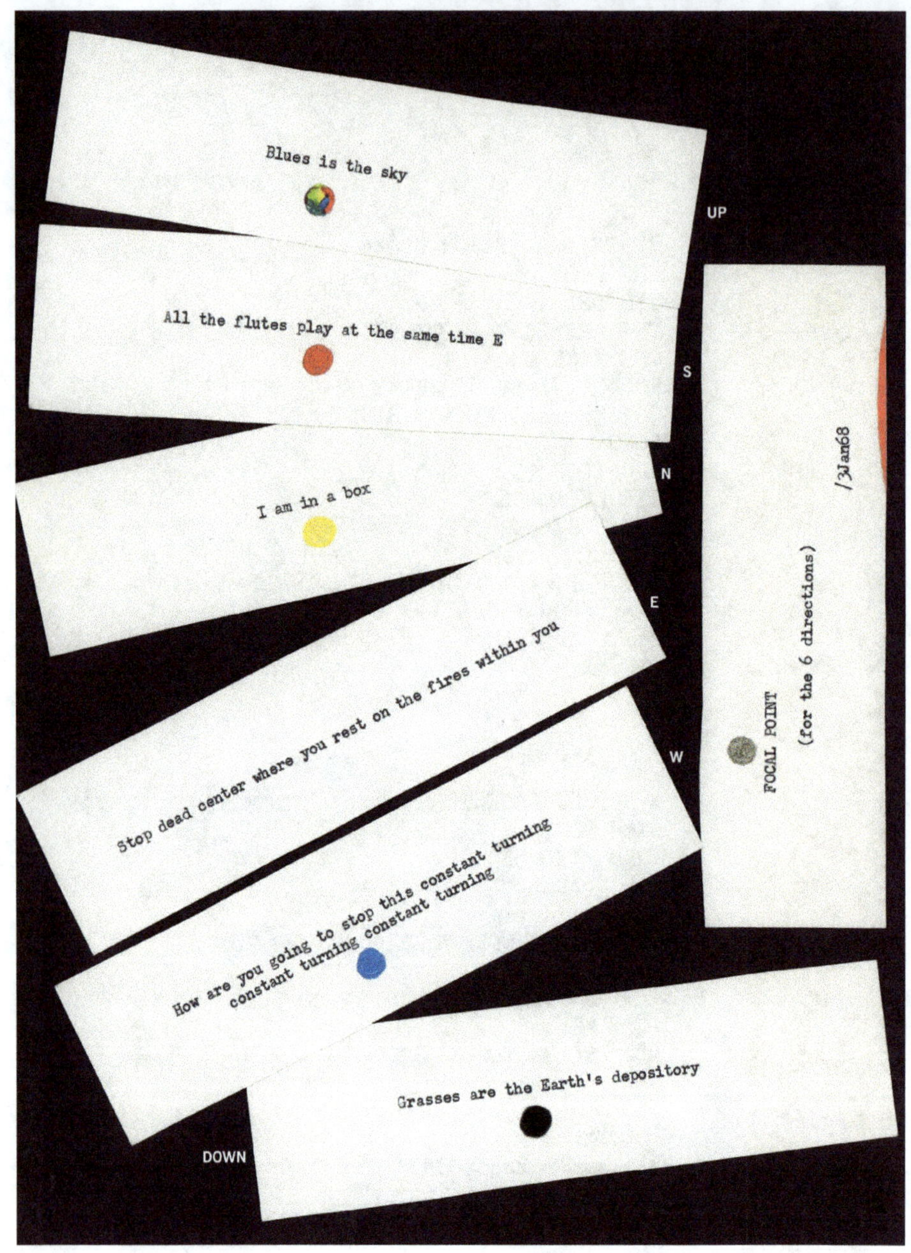

Cards in FOCAL POINT - In an empty room one card on center of each wall and ceiling and floor according to directions N E W S Up & Down. →

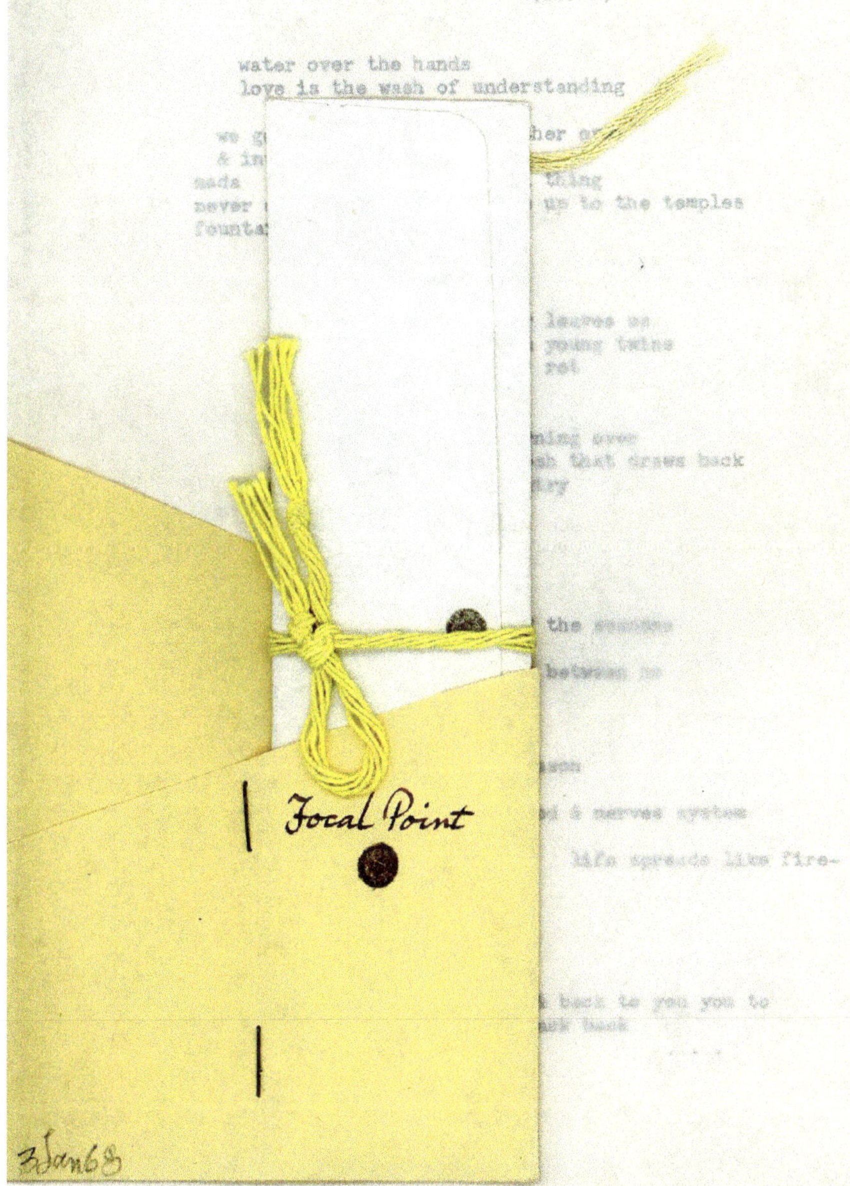
UNSPOKEN
(for M)
water over the hands
love is the wash of understanding
up to the temples
young twins
life spreads like fire-
Focal Point
3Jan68

UNSPOKEN

(for M)

water over the hands
love is the wash of understanding

we go   we go we   go together over
& into
nada   no thing   arise   all thing
never dies   dies   ever come up to the temples
fountains out from the eye

I am the third
of washing over
the dirt that never leaves us
earth   mother maiden young twins
boy   heart   twain   rot
baby go
we
arise in night time turning over
flame from the cold flesh that draws back
cringing from this country
afraid   to touch
the awful drawing back
or just

statement
I love you in the wash of the seasons

& rest on what moisture's between us
the acts of us
declare

-no voices of this winter season
our acts
fill in the roar of our blood & nerves system
none
rejoice in the anti-silence   life spreads like fire-

roar

unspoken

wave from me to you & back to you you to
back to you   back back back

. . .

God is a turbage factory

flame

spore

sun

dancing that hangs from the wrists

little men in nightgowns   run in to fight

end up jumping rope with paper dolls

complain
no more

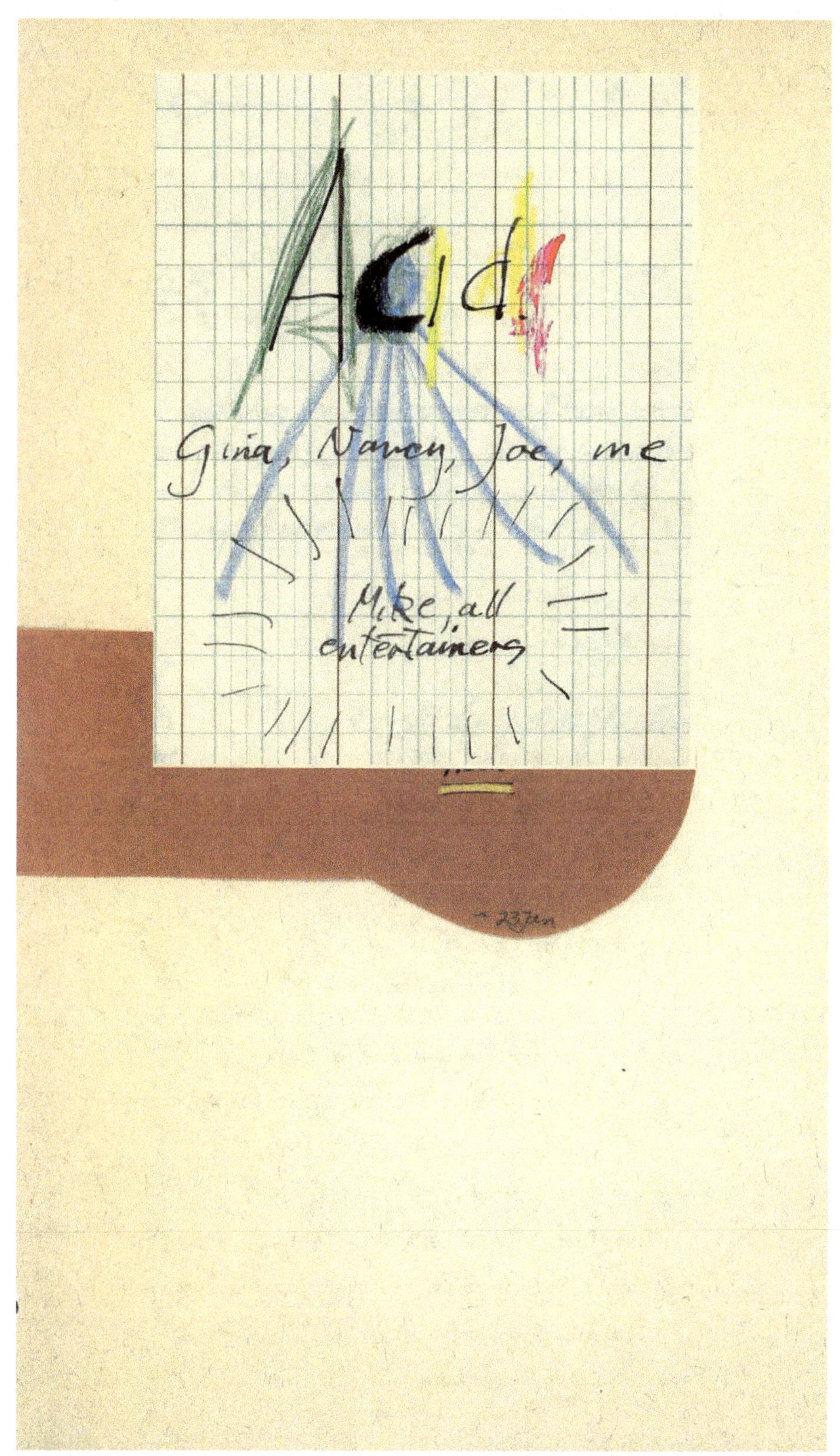
Acid
Gina, Nancy, Joe, me
Mike, all entertainers

THE GREEN THIEF

(listening to Carl Nielsen's Symphony #3)

the eyes of seeing are the eyes of green thieves

we come up in colors all the time

where in the rotated valve do we plunge ?

colors a stoppage

black & white is the stark gut

-hold me over the night-time of music-

abused in the color chart

-right times are forming-

the sacred Undine muse

gods of another name

*

there is no me only

the reference of emotion

quality of what I savor

the loss of you

I thot was my Saviour

returns me to me

colors dance
on the horizon

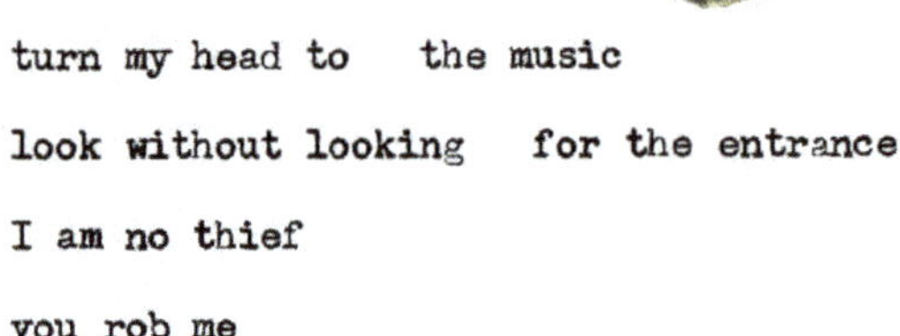

turn my head to the music

look without looking for the entrance

I am no thief

you rob me

leave me over the black & white graves

find myself here in the chair by the lamp

listening to Carl Nielsen's

Expansive Symphony

MIDI

Midi the extraordinary

dances

in a cabaret

where there is no time

Song of the Exterior Fold

I will catch you I will catch you
I will catch you catch you catch you

I will catch you I will catch you
I will catch you catch you catch you

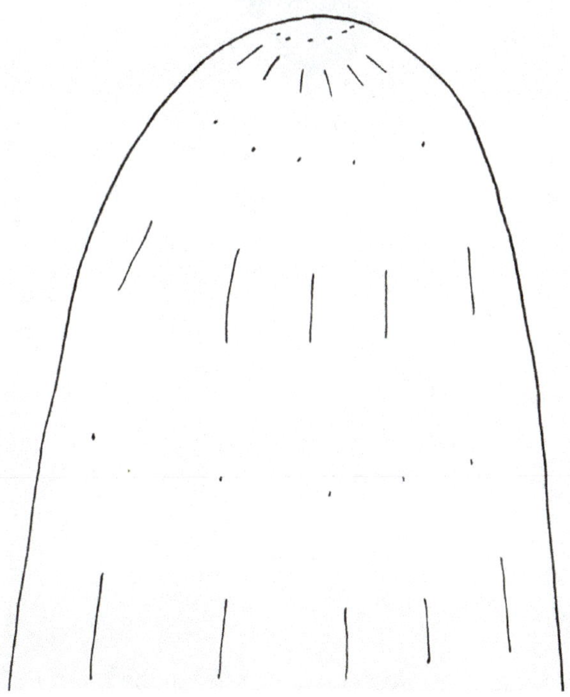

hand bound book (separate) made up of the following 5 poems

Caniptions in Fit Meter

knees

a love in the waste

no gaasit knock it
in the jaws & all

but affort two sisters
flow
Sarst

fess
flower up from

1

tie-
knees

a love in the waste

no gansit   knock it
in the jaws   & all

but effort   & two sisters
flow
Sarst

feast
flower up   from the feet

2

in time
to you
male a male

& the mind gone fond
of across

terraced where the wheat fields frozen
faster & faster

sun come up & gone down
a waste   acrossed

tear it up   & pull after

3

a going thru

walk off

is & isnt now

no
gal
is

but the wayfarer music magic tart tart

prepare   feast in the Injun sisters

walk off the mountain the brothers
are fasting

we bake together

in the prior sex teams

4

is it mind fastens,
a gonad shower

& equilibrium

love-
oo

stationmaster

lettuce she planted

hoe
sticks   in the garden tops

he in toes there

5

houses rub
each other   with doors & windows

our arms thru

a set in tone

wave of or-
ganism

gasm of use

neighbors   asleep in bed

A SET OF 4

A CASE OF POWER

screens
in the center of yr head

coils
stir them up

you broadcast

the love coil

man
size
wafer
onions in the sauce
my cinnamon
& yr Edam cheese

preparation
for star cast

2 friends over shells of   macaroni

where the Spirit draws down
to earth

the Wand for all time   to see   the Wafer of   just enough

set them vibrating
to the Universal Mind dance

the screen we look at anything   thru

dinner   the rain that came today
to return this land to the ocean

the flow   of our talking
sets the world in motion

& my words   love   in cases   speaks

FORCE WEED

it's all open

touch chords

where the ache is a-poppin   decomposition

thrives

the dance of the 2-man union

over a beer

I am going down   & then up   to where I am going down   & then up
spread yr circumstance across the world   the water that goes somewhere
till you are nothing

talk _into_

the last

chord

the Japanese   koto

Eto plays

we talk all afternoon

in the juices of structure

LORA / IN DELIGHT

into the delight you find me

woman   a core

of the apple I eat   in my mind
*
body is the flow of commitment
instant

& death of the past

*

eat of the flesh of you

& seeds come out my ears

delight you into find me

when we spark & times far

square   & pair

thank of you   yr purple hair

woman who
stuck in fruit

corn from mano   & metate

ground

spirits between us   .kiss

& delight comes out the ears

SET THEORY

3 stars for 4 more

how many friends will come & go

sets

cells

1 leads to another

molecule

baby

the color of my jackoff cream grey to green & blue beam

we all spread out in prism coats

lift our hips & jazz

softness into care

abandon the stars for a night
scene of love behind the mural set

I come up to say
I need David Gina Joe

the mind sets its own dance

to carry thru

& cartoons   wet their pants

who say it isnt so

THE HEARING

12

~~(the Last Supper)~~

the break   the thaw   the last snow   voices from the next room
it's true   is it not   now youve come before the hearing
the demarcation line is noble   the winter is a face   do you deny that>
or have yr constituents a better solution   anyone with a better plan>
shd come out of his hole in the snow & erupt upon the face of the earth
stress lines   we are the world of orange   you punch us on one side &>
we'll bulge all over   we've got to listen to our scientists
fuck the intellectuals   senator   watch yr language over the air
just stick to how we're going to withdraw our troops when the earth is>
shifting   the poles shifting   the rind of it   torn and bleeding
no spirit left in the people   squeeze functions   have terminated
face the panel and square yrself for the big news   what do you mean>
Mr. Secretary I am the news   do you wish to disturb the face of the earth>
with yr bitter attacks   we're swimming in orange juice
and you go around ordering malts   what have you, sir   check my record,
sir   I have, Mr. WeltSchmerz   have you any wool, sir
dont you think yr hair is a little too long   this is television
resort to reason when necessary   dont flounder around in the bushes
Madame, what are you doing on the scene   Im Suzy CreamCheese the>
Miracle Maiden   are you Exhibit A of false progress in the war
what do you mean war I simply give when Im taken   well watch yrself or>
you wont grow up like us   Sir Ive had my feet inspected and my hat's>
not on backwards   just because you have no taste dont accuse others>
of eating oranges   only one question at a time please   should we sustain
or call a smoke break   you may not smoke in front of the explosives
Sir, my soup is sour   do you expect me to eat this & talk at the>
same time   of course not this is an open hearing   take yr shoes off &>
illustrate yr approach   okay okay that leaves me with one more thing>
to say   if you want to be peaceful, be peaceful

(excerpt) wrote Chapter 12 of A New Land

SONG FOR SPRING
& THE UNION OF OPPOSITE MEN

sing for the many   reunions

go all the way where you are pushed

off

    float   2 in the sky pitcher

fields of particles   move   nearer

until their heads interlock   & without turning

flow out of each other

        age difference   lop over

        dawn

      between us   18   32

       & you love   so

  much

you talk to hear somebody <u>e</u>lse think

feel great manna   the coil   giving

give back

so much taking friendship   launches

springtime

THE FEAST OF DREAMS

(for J. sleeping)

sleep   the record at the end
a slow   drifting   machine

*

you are lost   & the waves ripple under you

*

babies
& ice cream

*

sleep   I live out the state where you breathe
& enter
you lie back on   the table of the world
& lift it
I cannot move

Sagitarian   Priest   who sleeps

the leaders have dissolved into lovers
& lie back   for the feast

the light that is forever in our dreams

fall

pick up in triangle   sun from the window

curtains

blanket   it falls on   ever raised

walking thru the pyramids

time in f_a_iling order

no time,

a ball

EVOLUTION A TROIS

all those human animals
in the blood

cryptogamous plants

heterosexual motorcycles

apes riding them
out of the swamps

Poetry Performance Dance featuring Bill Pearlman, Meredith Rice (poster), Mel Buffington, Larry Goodell and Gandalf

4 POEMS

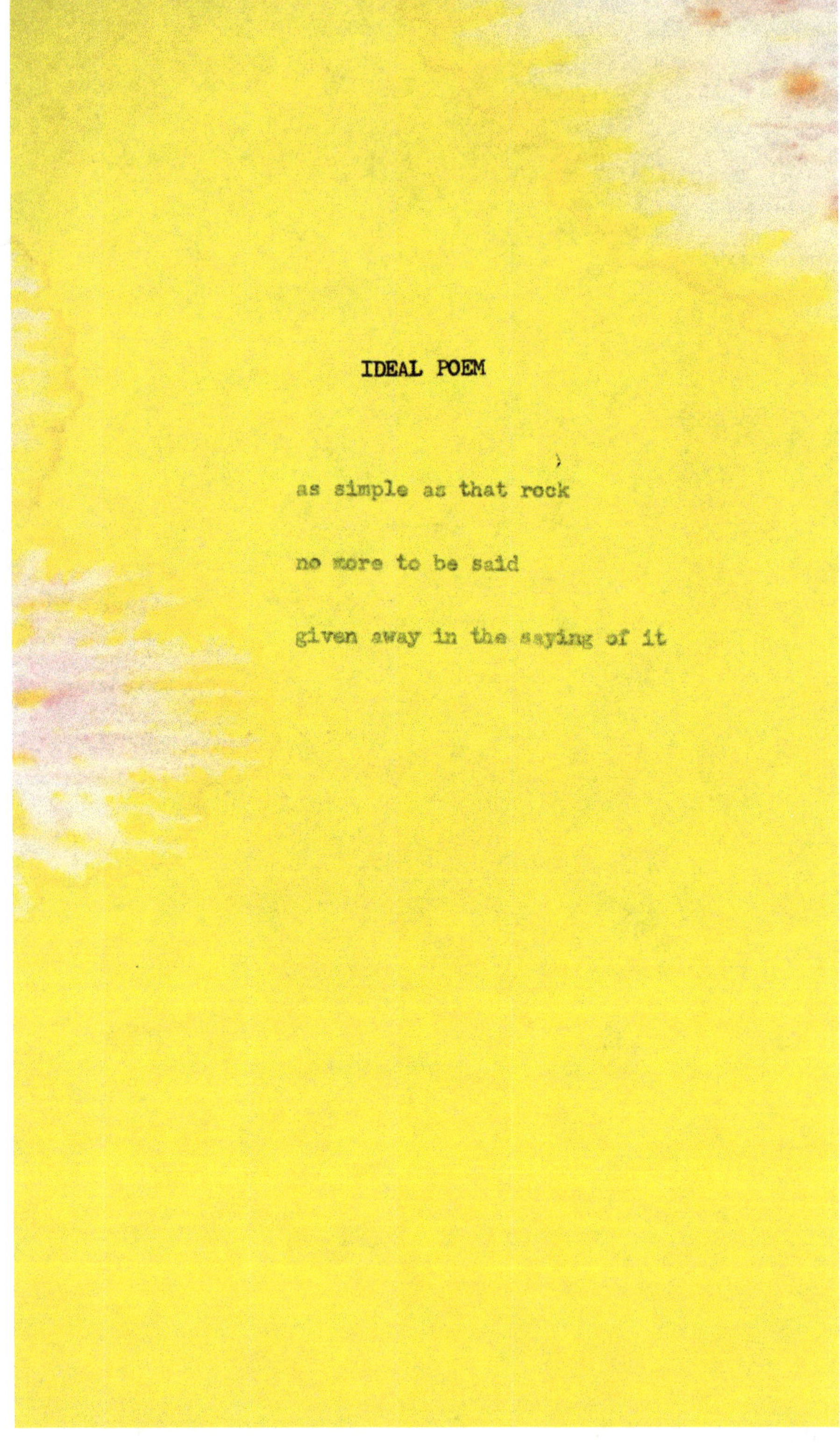

IDEAL POEM

as simple as that rock

no more to be said

given away in the saying of it

as simple as that rock

no more to be said

given away in the saying of it

SONG

Sing to the heart of things

stay there

[illegible] tied in it

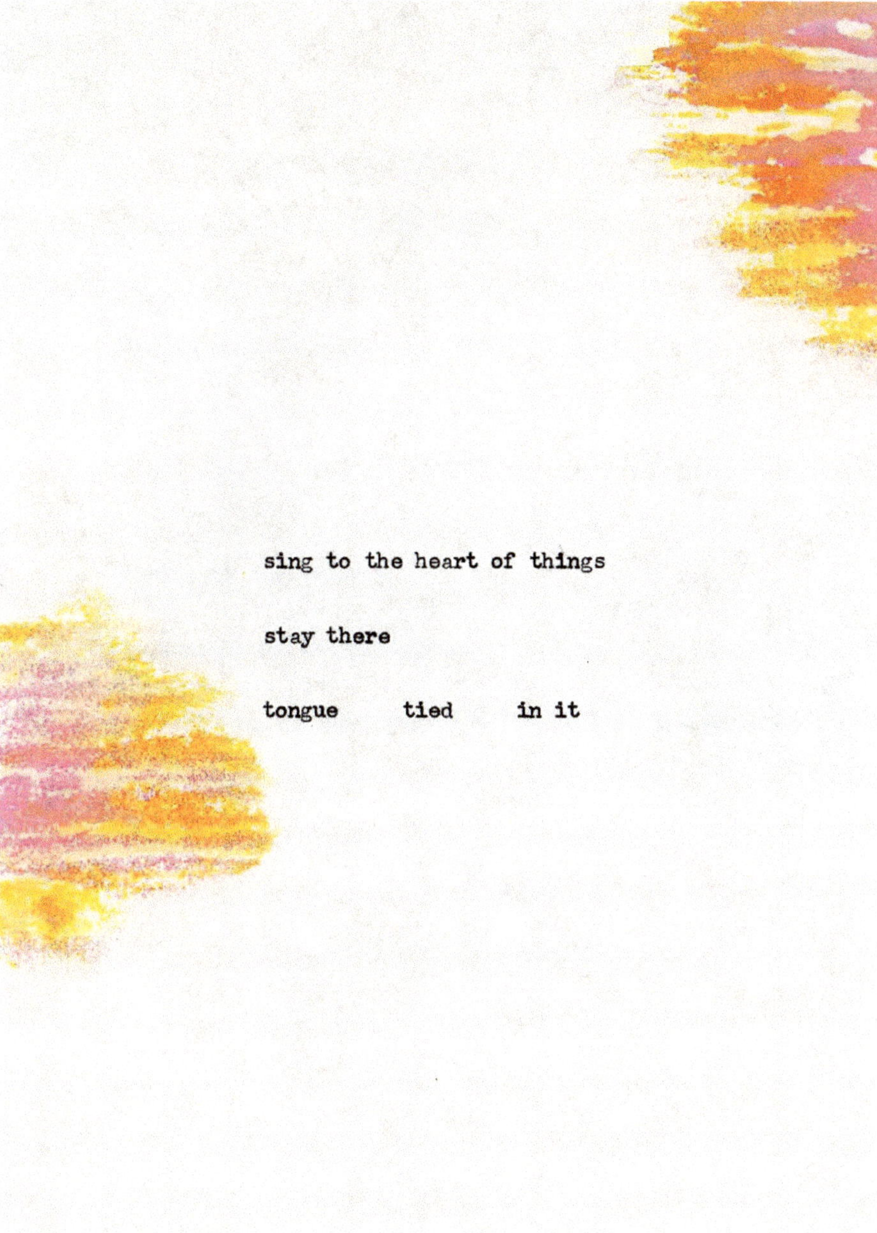

sing to the heart of things

stay there

tongue   tied   in it

DREAM

doorway to the reverse

the asshole of the primitive

water flowing up the arroyos to the top of the mountain

doorway to the reverse

the asshole of the primitive

water flowing up the arroyos to the top of the mountain

A SILENCE

no talk where shared carried
over to you said
that way

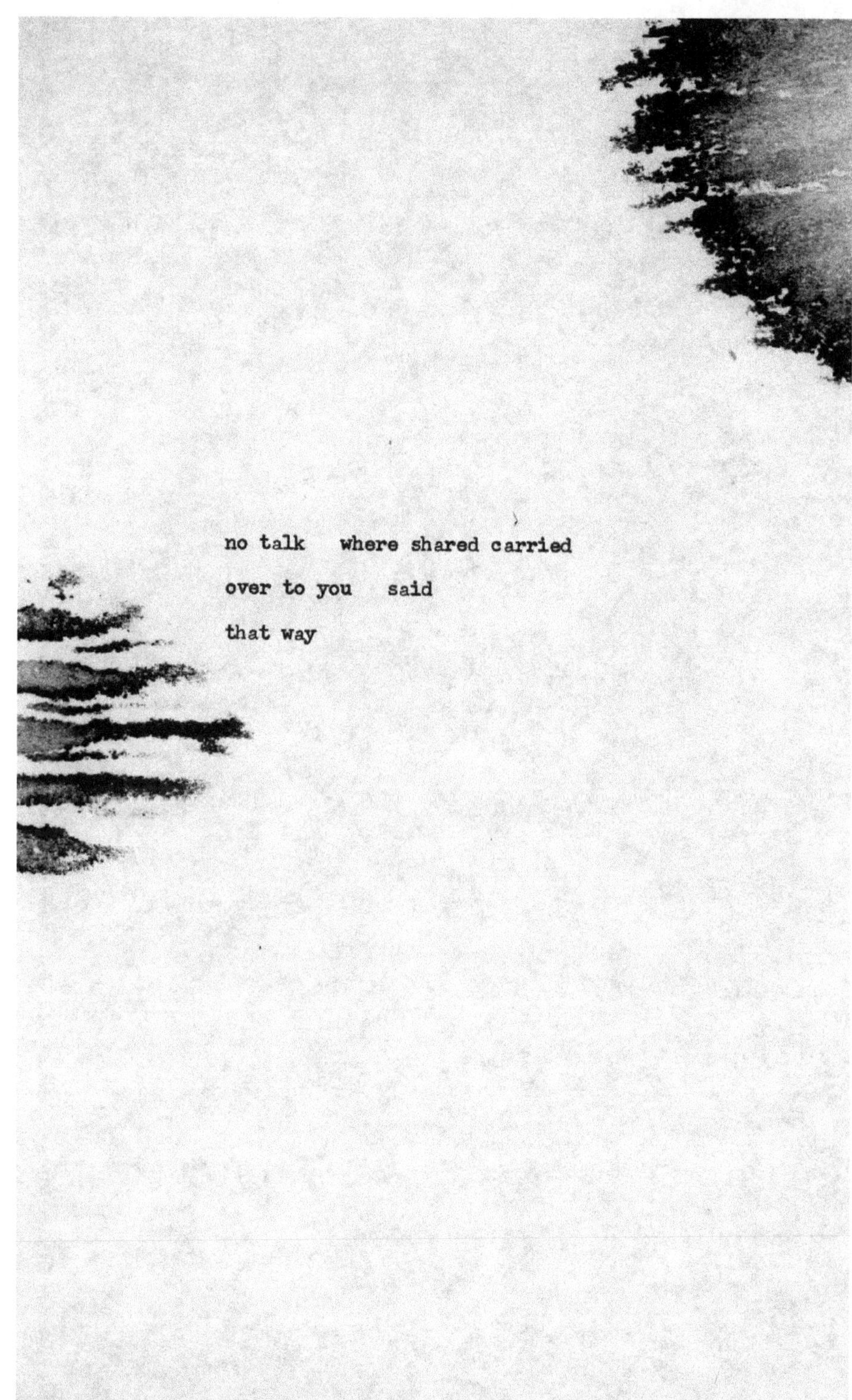

no talk   where shared carried

over to you   said

that way

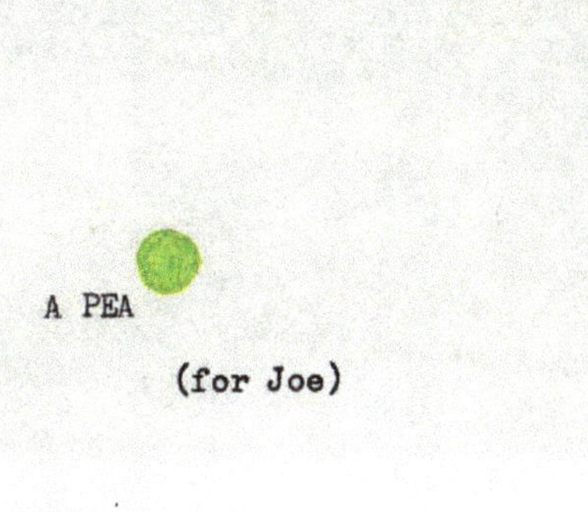

A PEA

(for Joe)

shitty closed bad

violence reek on

fester to reach its apoplectic ultimate piss-out
RIP OFF ANTLERS

bitty mosed glad

strip of silver in the sky rain forecast

umination of a stripped car *

ing hollow

around with chicken feathers on in our dreams

OUR DREAMS

OPEN UP MOTHERFUCKER

y on here by the fireplace waiting for somebody else

stay on here planting things

I-THOU

terms with a meat-cleaver the statement is made

it grinds the sentences out into words

death in violence state up the ass

till it's the size of a pea (this whole country & all the shit of it)

I eat it

illumination of a stripped car / body reeking / hollow / walk around with chicken feathers on / in our dreams / IN OUR DREAMS / OPEN UP MOTHERFUCKER / stay on here by the fireplace waiting for somebody else

ON THE MOUNTAIN

13<postlude>

the world lost   a new land gained   gains & losses in coins   hills

flat land

a simple order of speech is an asset   mark it blue

the sky the silver sat upon

a genie without a master   floats by

Come down   bring me something I cant define   YOU   MASTER

CANNOT DEFINE   PUT YR HANDS ON MY SHOULDERS   I WILL CARRY YOU OVER

a simple command,   Stay in my hands awhile

carried on the strength >

of this mountain,   everywhere I am is movement   the eyes rest on>

the corner of something   and it is the corner of the world

I sail thru the floating   counter-balanced molecules

& sail back out again   in the flux of more   I want more all the time

the road in the moon   up and down and then up more and down and then >

the downs are exalted over   the downs there were before

when you started out   I started out being spanked for spilling

chocolate milk on the kitchen floor   I didnt do it   or now

what happened   you dont forget anything?   or do you forget it all

there are blanks that pulsate   plates of silver over the sky &

I float on the giant's mountain shoulder   each hair there   a tree

the blank plates   with no words written on them   the eternal

memory

the only limitation   is the threshold to the world

as I am carried on the shoulders   the breathing mountain

the plates in the sky open up   two great silvers   carry   moisture

the threshold to high is a diaphragm   opening   subtle closing

I read as it closes,   what closes it?   what brings the intermission time

the down   hill   the giant is not a giant at all

but is a mountain under me   and I am the giant/midget   no size

only proportion

(excerpt) wrote postlude of A New Land

THE CIRCUMSCRIBED GENERATION (or)
LOVE SONG FOR GINO, KEN, KELL, ANN, etc. ETC.

alive in the wail

tangents given

FUCK YR CIRCLE
(circle back to me)
con FURSHUN fessin I buv oo

pookypoopookee
STOPPER
& HE CDNT
STOPPER
(plug out the wrench)
WENCH
!
oldfashioned syndrome of loneliness
a bugger up the ass
Old
fortune
card up the
HEARING AID ?

LISTEN TO MY QUESTION
BLOODWORT

No

poem folded up

THE CIRCUMSCRIBED GENERATION (or)
LOVE SONG FOR GINO, KEN, KELL, ANN, etc. ETC.

alive in the wail

tangents given

FUCK YR CIRCLE
(circle back to me)
con FURSHUN fessin I buv oo

pookypoopookee
STOPPER
& HE CDNT
STOPPER
(plug out the wrench)
WENCH
!
oldfashioned syndrome of loneliness
a bugger up the ass
Old
fortune
card up the
HEARING AID ?

LISTEN TO MY QUESTION
BLOODWORT

No
Resentment
Only

o lover o o o

MEASLES
COO/COO
AHI-AHI

(Clear Yr Throat
Drambuie
Cough Up Yr Honey
& Git DRUNK

hi?
hi?
hi?

I'm a slow phase locked in eternal union

diga me
toot?

top part of fold out

Tootsie Hardon.

Direct me
Old-Fashioned Master
I
shd
upstage you all the time ?

I'm hummm
ble
HERBERT STOP PICKING YR TEETH

Mother
I dont
have
any teeth youve
sucked
them
all
oft!

PEESQUEEZE!!!!!!!!

Yr
lost
little girl.
I
period
come
back
again
period
WE
I say from the self-circumscribed circle
old bandit in Wolf drag
WE
codger drunk-dodger lickety split tap dancer
& herbert fondler
SINS-INSURED
WE
dig me
hard
WE
COME
BACK

(ha-ha-ha-ha-ha-)
WE
(dusty fingertips)
WE
COME
BACK

TO
LIFE!!!!!!!!!!!!

bottom part of fold out

Man Hooded

~~a bitch — take that~~
~~shout her with cum~~
~~& hope she has a baby~~

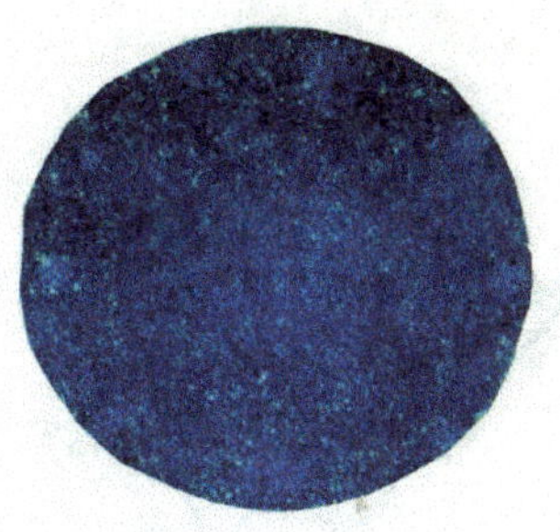

an offshoot of space

rediscovering delight

there is a blue
there is a blue
plate
in the window

light shines thru

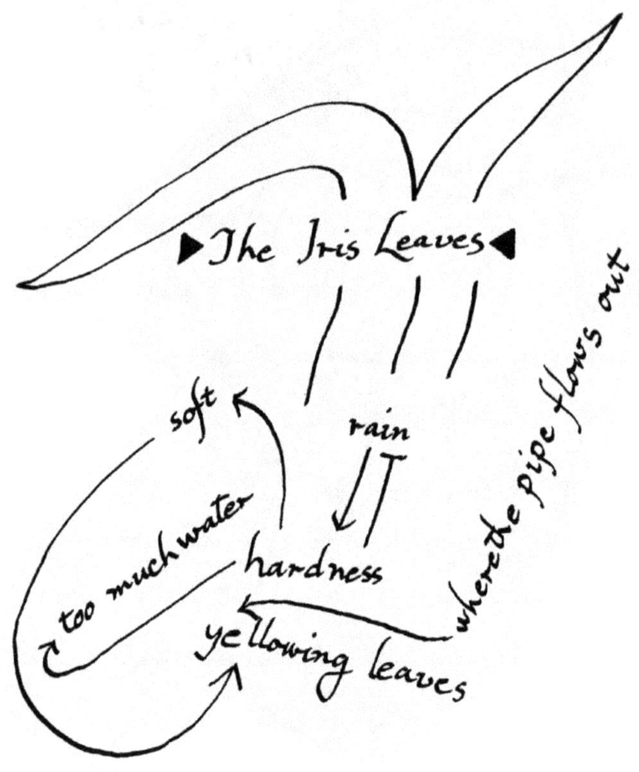
The Iris Leaves
soft
rain
too much water
hardness
where the pipe flows out
yellowing leaves

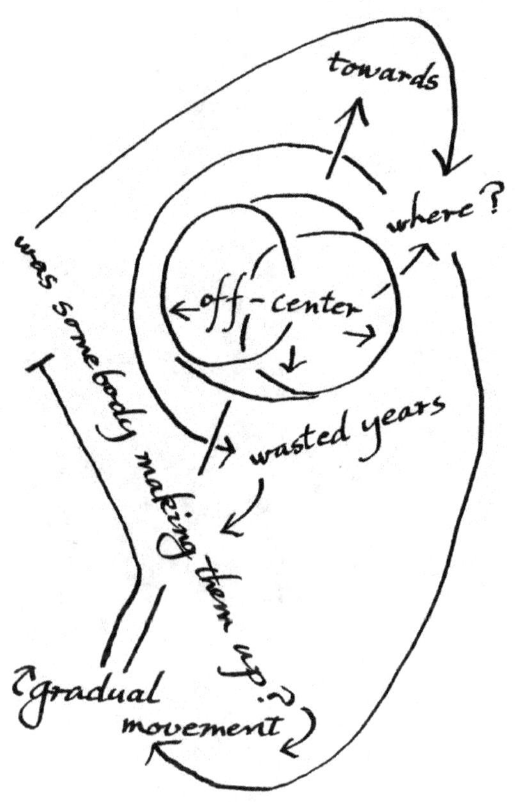
towards
where?
off-center
wasted years
was somebody making them up?
gradual movement

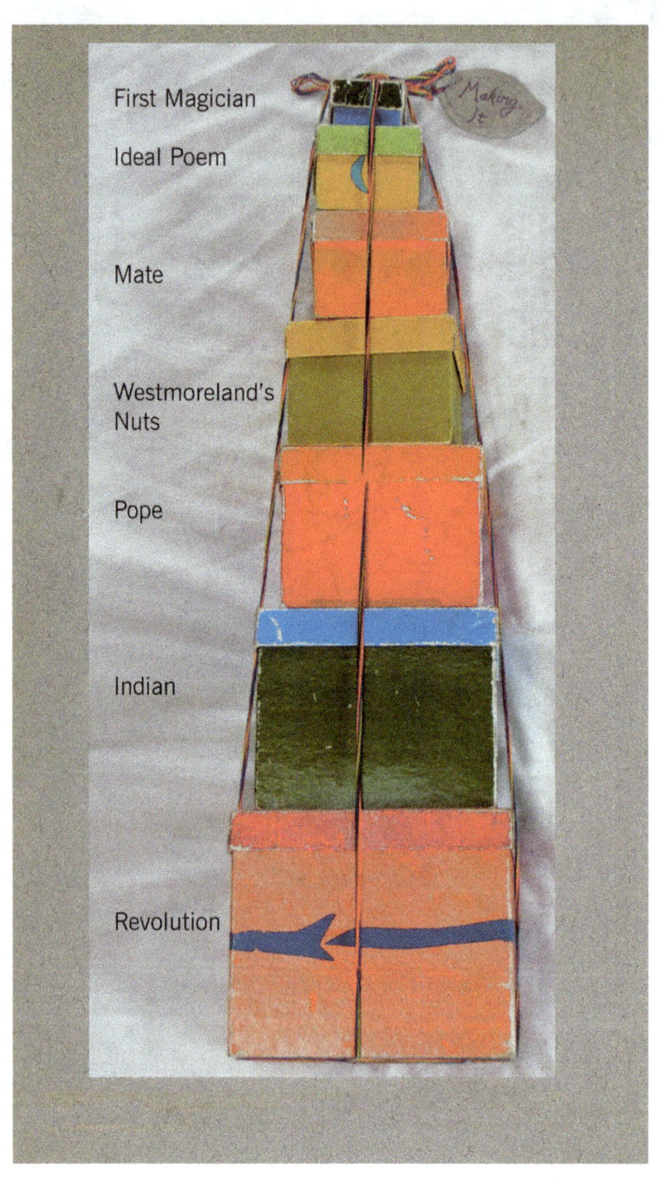

Making It - box poems about aspects of poetry created - see page 104

ENTRANCE

I was driving down the side of the world   literally
driving down the side of the world

when everything fell off   formed its own landscape   in front of me
I drove down on

JEWEL

it's a beautiful note that sings on where the patterns of stress wave

~~wave stress patterns where sings note beautiful it is~~xxxxxxxxxxx
word

constellation of age

young in
young enough

I am generated   generation   jeweLLLLLLLLLLLLLLLLLLLLLLLL**AHHHHHHHHHH**!

Photograph by Mel Buffington, Kiva Auditorium UNM

The Fool created 22 May - *see page 111*

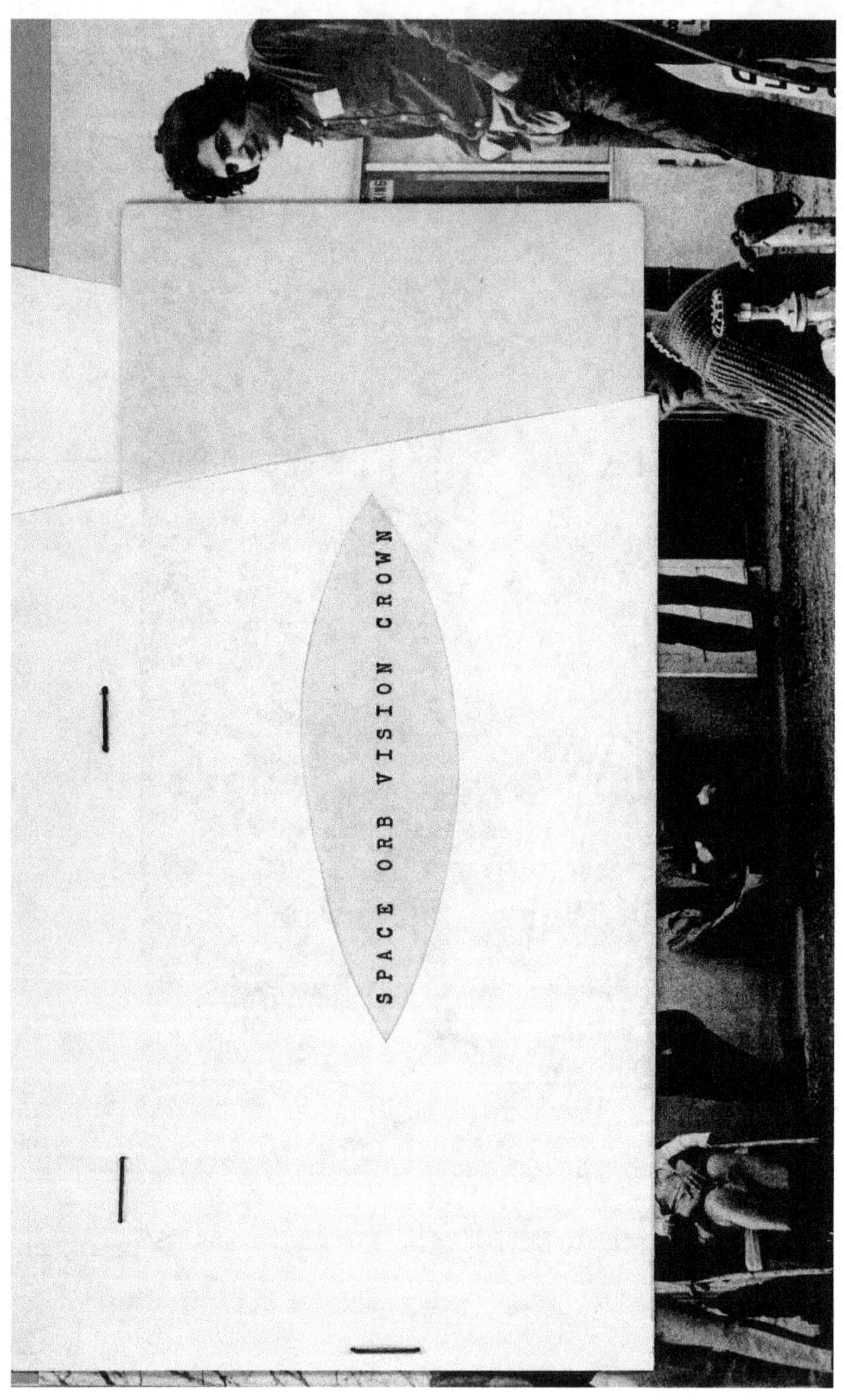

accordion fold wedding poem

S P A C E O R B V I S I O N C R O W N

(for Joe & Olivia, June 1, Wedding)

orb in & space divides in union   time square & nipples touch

love fall down get up help again
follow the bridges up & down
between the stars & the sun

SUN DIVIDES
THE RIGHT FROM RIGHT

touch kindly souls   where the square past is a fool

dull nuggets
dull nuggets
dull nuggets
dull nuggets

wake up in a mineral bed
fucked 3 Xs from toe to head

out forecast out spinning out
sun out forecast spinning out
out sun forecast spinning out
sun out sun out spinning out
sun out forecast spinning out

holiday for sap origins
trees dancing
seeds sprouted dancing
root fetishes   dancing

the right
woman right
the right
man the right
woman right
man right
man right
woman right
man the right
woman right
man woman right

love centered out love Joe Olivia centered out
love Olivia centered Joe love Olivia centered out
love Olivia love Olivia love Olivia centered out
love Joe Olivia love Joe love centered out

S P A C E   O R B   V I S I O N   C R O W N

T H E   F O O L

the world is entry   intrigue   dynamite

messages in paper bags descended from the sun

arguments are unnecessary   I love you
arguments are unnecessary   I love you

ha.

echo chamber

a garden in the wind

no mind to find wife with

heart   blood

coercion of distances

where is the self   made   mate

nothing in the world in my pants but my pants on

gasket   a screw   a happy mechanic

THE AMERICAN PARTY

deny me deny me   solace for dreams   ?
walking on spaces   with my hands tied
towels robes of color in the bathroom
come out to the bash of party drunk on stp
stop bang curry mustard   FISH   FISH
velvet underground
walk in somebody's arms
everything the American dream   here?
back up against the radiator   wondering   steam
in the city   lush night   Albuquerque no city stuck
on the landscape   hollyhocks growing around me
all in a turnip wad spat out spinach & radishes
grown in the garden

a garden in the wind   vision a friend had gun pointed to him
GET OUT YOU HUPPIE   left with friends
things scattered in the rusty trailor by the creek
overlooking the farm rows he worked hoping
enough for everybody

hand out free vegetables things at Sandia
Corporation where they store the bombs
anyplace

gone like pigeons   mind pecked at   thin
body   to touch a friend   when lights drove up

scattered us   recent busts   hiding beer cans in the car
worried about a little box of hash-piece
codpieces off   I dropped out of the city   stoned back
in the shell   being
eaten   everybody wasted gone   fucking in rooms sorrowing
outside

-is it true   old notions of hay dreams
what is a party   make it with the captain of the ship
the hay maiden   peppermint schnaps & rock & roll
somebody told me   your ears are split
two-toed   dancing around inside me   satyr-devils
tying ribbons around my soul   offer it to the stone
driveway outside   the floor   bottom that falls out
dancing tying me to the car seat   out under a window
noise of touch   drone comes down   split take off-
vision   virgin-shit
vision   nightmare for half-asses   pebbles
pasted over their faces
vision   the horse is inside you and calls you ugly
while I'm around the corner looking for a lit door
to knock on

space

give me voice for turn-on   fried rabbits   itch where two lever-legs
come together   other people touching, the hermit
assumes the half-lotus
& waits for converts
Buddhas   people the Sandias   look out over the city which has just as
serenely   disappeared
skin & bones
skin & bones
you dont know yr name again
eats you
space in somebody else's garden to sit & watch
dynamite under my feet & the last match in my pocket

dis → cord

THE FOOL

I will track down my vision
find it isnt true
go over the edge of the cliff
& hit the blue.

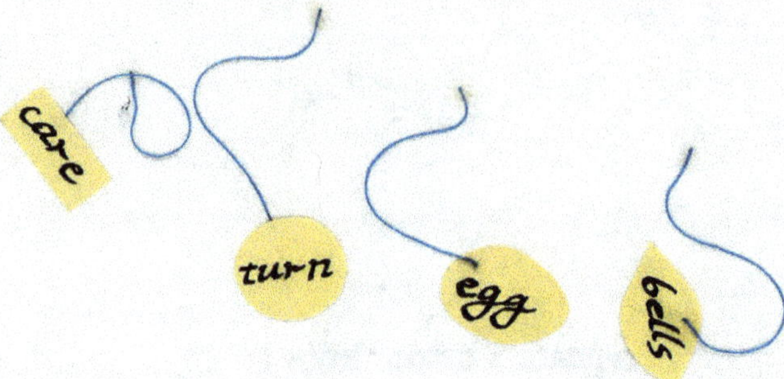
care
turn
egg
bells

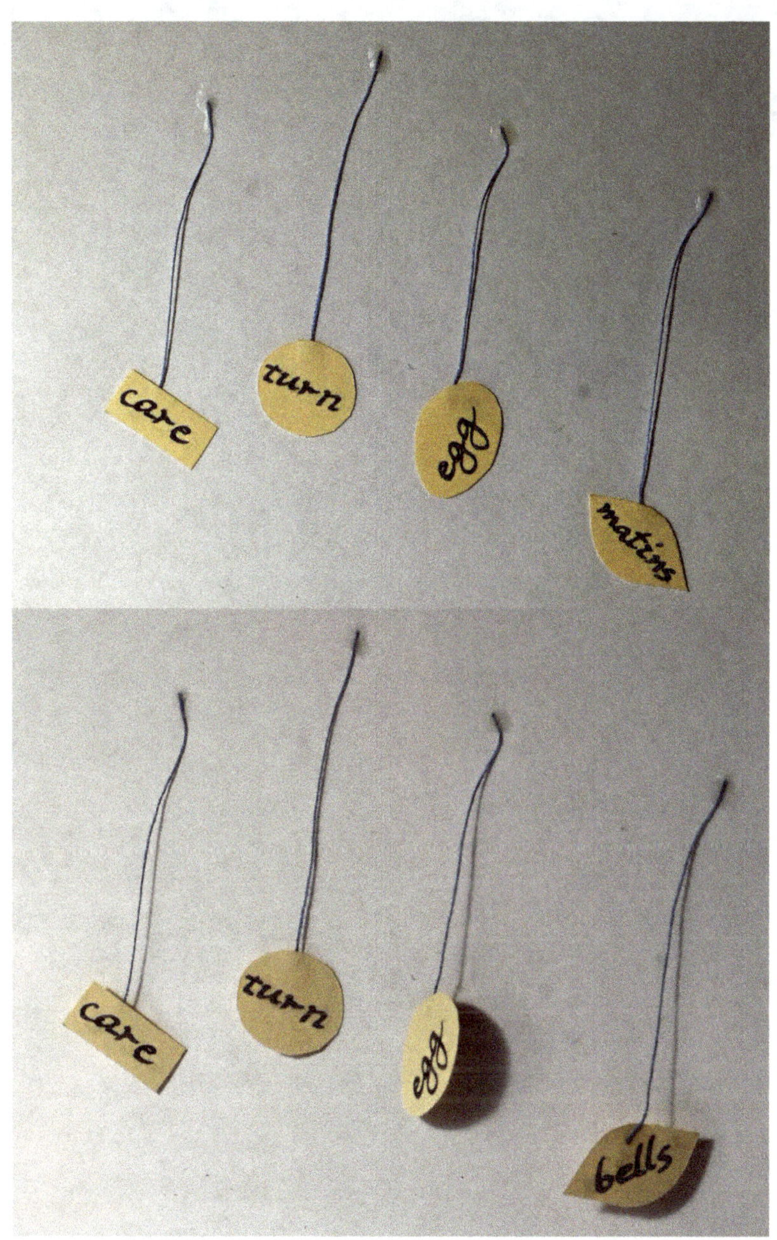

←

views of "Dangling Poem" for Olivia

3 POEMS AROUND A BIRTHDAY

hate is a vineyard   noble rocks & gorges formed

I will sit on this tree   & announce to the flowers
that anybody can come

grapes or no grapes

I love a man & I love any woman

& the sky squeezes me   hard

(strawberries cover the neck where
the men lay on the rocks & talked about
not making (love)

hold thy heart in blazes

four square

couple fucking in the other room

    is that why we are   opposite   kind   ?

    to come in one another   no   desire   ?

I answer all   & I answer   nothing

—— —— —— —— ——

blazes   rafters   ridge-pole sings

SONG

stone cutters   fly

meet in the arc-house of Methusala

wanna-galla

rainbow is Her tongue   She wags it thru the gardens
of the universe
burst of dishes
the household on fire

stone cutters   fly

meet in the arc-house of Methusala

wanna-galla

rainbow is Her tongue   She wags it thru the gardens
of the universe

CORRIDOR OUT

  electric fires   gone off the ridge
where we settle our complaints
in bed
in the head   the toes freeze
corridors of temples   in ice
multifacet
        molecular colors
      lead me on

in her arms   lead me on
the reverse of the temple
multifaceted as the moon

the artifacts fall out   slide off the magician's table

on her bed
my bed   mine of the earth

get up at dawn in   the dream of the dream
where the entrance is never barred

-for Lenore

mugwump little daisies in our only meadow
between the crow caws & the birds I cdnt see so high
making love

spiral down into a framework dome
erected in a valley for summer solstice
wedding ashram mugwump hog farm
generators buzzing freak out sorceror
dancing --
panels of white cloth up light show
blown 3 sails in the wind
gathering in New Mexico mountains
bonfire hog horse & cowboy blues
womped in cup of hills

between us only fire

dancers lifting in the wind
bodies in rapid
heave below

a couple married in blankets flying down the hill into
flying down the hill

love devil ramp

to catch & carry from us yarrow/pot smokes or not
what lives except in the sanctity of death

but in a circle where we go in & out --

Clarity is the breath of angels.

SCULPTRESS OF THE CALENDAR STONE

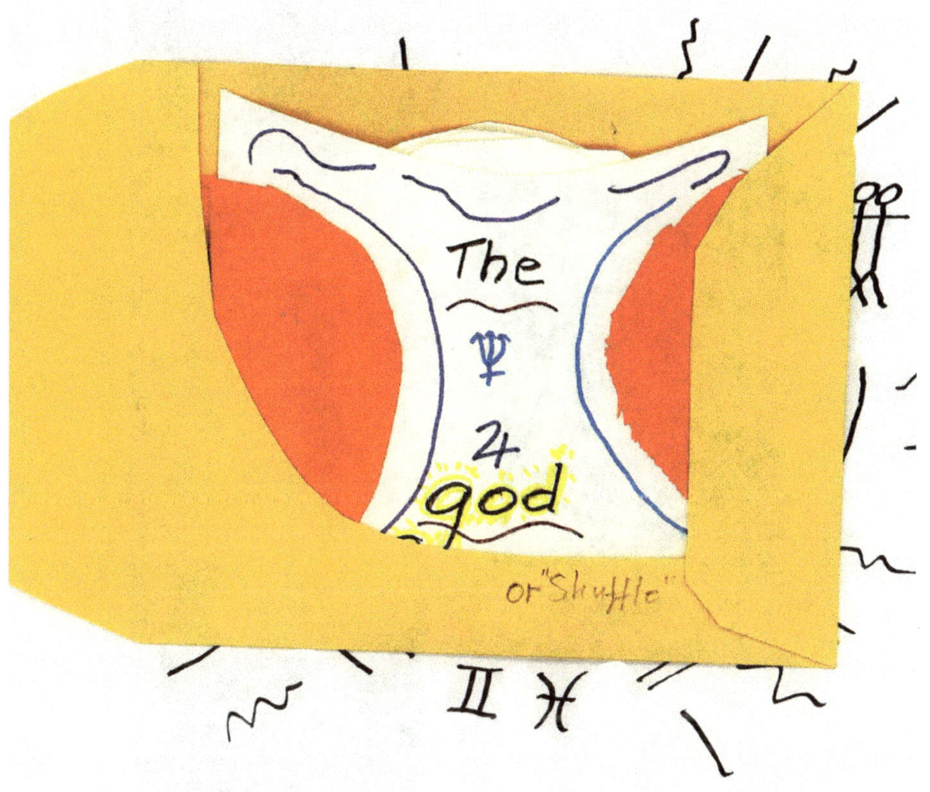

"The God," shuffle poem for Dick Hanson

legs
round
tiny
feels
alive
arms
heart
flower
solid
sing
friendship
soup
barrier
body
shuffle & read
one color
turn over, read
the other
OR
shuffle getting colors mixed
UP
& read

the god

diagram of set up for meditation in sand, Chalchalacas

SCULPTRESS OF THE CALENDAR STONE

go lovely
girl into white origins
where the rain falls under me
& I lie on the calendar   floating
with my prick in the center of you

LEAF FROM A FALLING TREE

Hello God   how is it up there   ?

where no one speaks English

HITLER HAD ONE (1) TESTICLE

MUDHEAD SONG

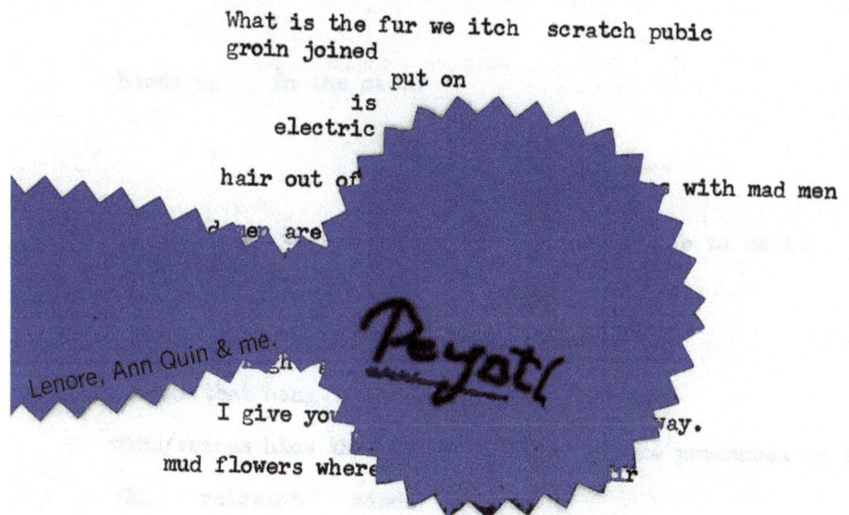

MUDHEAD SONG

What is the fur we itch scratch pubic
groin joined
put on
is
electric --

hair out of the head communicates with mad men

mud men are incestuous &
love their duties

dance after sunset

night goodies for the feast --

I give you my peyote day to take away.

mud flowers where we touch our hair

A SET OF LOOK-THRUS FOR 3-DIMENSIONAL VISION

•

hands up   in the mazes

•

the ceilings that fall from the sky are grace to be in

•

things that hang   are emblems
wind/voices blow thru them   friends whose presences we are
all   relevant   minds
entrances
here

•

(shower of sparks where pen point touches the paper & moves

DEAR GOD

MY HEART IS SOD

MY PRAYER IS ROD

Q?

0 why God stars again

1 ~ all sound

2 sun star stone plant animal man god

3 ~ a gash

4 the center of a city

5 all known things

6 ~ sleep

7 ~ we'll have supper at 8

9 ~ turning

in digits . power

the powers work thru a moving focus

THE COUPLE

with paradise to come   she was gaining admittance
while he sat there   waiting for more

sing in possession of yr soul in possession of yr song

petroglyph Washington State

W A R   G A M E

RAW (place on square 9)

given actions pursuit follows

WAR (on square 6)

the grease monkey bluts groin in tore fashion
a
MERICAMIXUP

GLUE on square 2

GOING is the roving backfielder

(raw glue liquid flue)

dis ease (square 3 & 8 joined)

attachment to the heart, square 1

on 10 no word Miss Tickle '68
a square with nothing in it
a playing board continually moving that is
from yr lap

WAR GAMES repeat backwards & move 3 spaces

1 set up light housekeeping
2 autumn winds blow the whole town down
3 you have arrived retreat 2 men dig their fingers into
each other's navels
interrupt yr vision

option
I have none

Sorry, you lost toss the dice
the twin with the orange face wins

a raw war goes gluing on backwards in ease
somebody else's
somebody else's ?

clap board
history beyond the tracks his
body rejected the heart
somebody else's ?

'

you hit square 4
BUILD A TOWN

there is a big fat cunt on square 5
to be tucked in as you move the playing board
back on yr lap

scratch it there

RAW VISION 7 7

go Thou forward taking leaving
enter do not knock

(walls have ears & eyes & glue liquid flue
smoke bomb

square 8 unrevealed no
speech for it words fail

the screaming acid city haunts me
bombs fall pyramids
molt

11 11 11

a dried up caterpillar in the window

cross jab under pinning forfeit
nothing
sickness
of what seeps thru the walls

eyes of the dead game of the dead come to say nothing do
nothing thing
amajig

magic square moves
perception/inter
ception of the whole world
10 feet tall

go forward reverse lights flashing going
is coming back you win the war
RAW glue
5
argues with the umpire

you come sailing out of the cunt
to accept yr prize

a fist around the water
that feeds the whole town

BUT IS

it was it is but was it is it was it is but was it is

it is but was it is or was it is but was it is or was

no longer was but is it is no longer was but is it is

it was it is no longer was but is no longer was but is

for Sandy (Harris) Clarke

LIFESAVER

cheese is particular to dumplings
dumplings are particular to knees
knees are particular to assholes
assholes are particular to Mother's Oats
Mother's Oats is particular to daffodils
daffodils are particular to Alaska
Alaska is particular to Maine
Maine is particular to britches
britches are particular to soap suds
soap suds are particular to Norway
Norway is particular to Africa
Africa is particular to dinner tables
dinner tables are particular to funeral wreaths
funeral wreaths are particular to pianos
pianos are particular to middle class
middle class is particular to barber poles
barber poles are particular to Spudnuts
Spudnuts are particular to dandelions
dandelions are particular to people
people are particular to butter
butter is particular to hydrogenated fats
hydrogenated fats are particular to mothballs
mothballs are particular to Mark Twain
Mark Twain is particular to Suzy Cream Cheese
Suzy Cream Cheese is particular to wide ties
wide ties are particular to zoot suits
zoot suits are particular to paranoia
paranoia is particular to toilet seats
toilet seats are particular to wrist watches
wrist watches are particular to candied gum
candied gum is particular to Winesburg, Ohio
Winesburg, Ohio is particular to Chicago

folded poem based on an expression by Robert Creeley➜

cheese is particular to dumplings ←*start here*
dumplings are particular to knees
knees are particular to assholes
assholes are particular to Mother's Oats
Mother's Oats is particular to daffodils
daffodils are particular to Alaska
Alaska is particular to Maine
Maine is particular to britches LIFESAVER
britches are particular to soap suds
soap suds are particular to Norway
Norway is particular to Africa
Africa is particular to dinner tables
dinner tables are particular to funeral wreaths
funeral wreaths are particular to pianos
pianos are particular to middle class
middle class is particular to barber poles
barber poles are particular to Spudnuts
Spudnuts are particular to dandelions
dandelions are particular to people
people are particular to butter
butter is particular to hydrogenated fats
hydrogenated fats are particular to mothballs
mothballs are particular to Mark Twain
Mark Twain is particular to Suzy Cream Cheese
Suzy Cream Cheese is particular to wide ties
wide ties are particular to zoot suits
zoot suits are particular to paranoia
paranoia is particular to toilet seats
toilet seats are particular to wrist watches
wrist watches are particular to candied gum
candied gum is particular to Winesburg, Ohio
Winesburg, Ohio is particular to Chicago
Chicago is particular to ice cream
ice cream is particular to handsome is as handsome does
handsome is as handsome does is particular to no one
no one is particular to Odysseus
Odysseus is particular to Rebel
Rebel is particular to hound dogs
hound dogs are particular to friends
friends are particular to novocaine
novocaine is particular to pharmacists
pharmacists are particular to drop outs
drop outs are particular to Cashmere Bouquet
Cashmere Bouquet is particular to fleur-de-lis
fleur-de-lis is particular to down home
down home is particular to water witching
water witching is particular to mixed nuts
mixed nuts are particular to no man's land
no man's land is particular to sky diving

no man's land is particular to sky diving
sky diving is particular to water reefs
water reefs are particular to lighthouses
lighthouses are particular to trimming trees
trimming trees is particular to Prokofiev
Prokofiev is particular to the United States
the United States is particular to taking a bath as opposed to taking a shower
taking a bath as opposed to taking a shower is particular to raisins
raisins are particular to good diet
good diet is particular to catching a cold
catching a cold is particular to everyone
everyone is particular to glaciers
glaciers are particular to dictionaries
dictionaries are particular to how the world turns round
how the world turns round is particular to the death moan
the death moan is particular to ant hills
ant hills are particular to alcoholism
alcoholism is particular to the moving finger
the moving finger is particular to what are you going to put on the phonograph now
what are you going to put on the phonograph now is particular to my kind of gal
my kind of gal is particular to Life magazine
Life magazine is particular to old issues
old issues are particular to small apartments
small apartments are particular to old friends
old friends are particular to getting something going
getting something going is particular to getting there on time
getting there on time saves lives

end of unfolded poem

back page of "Lifesaver"

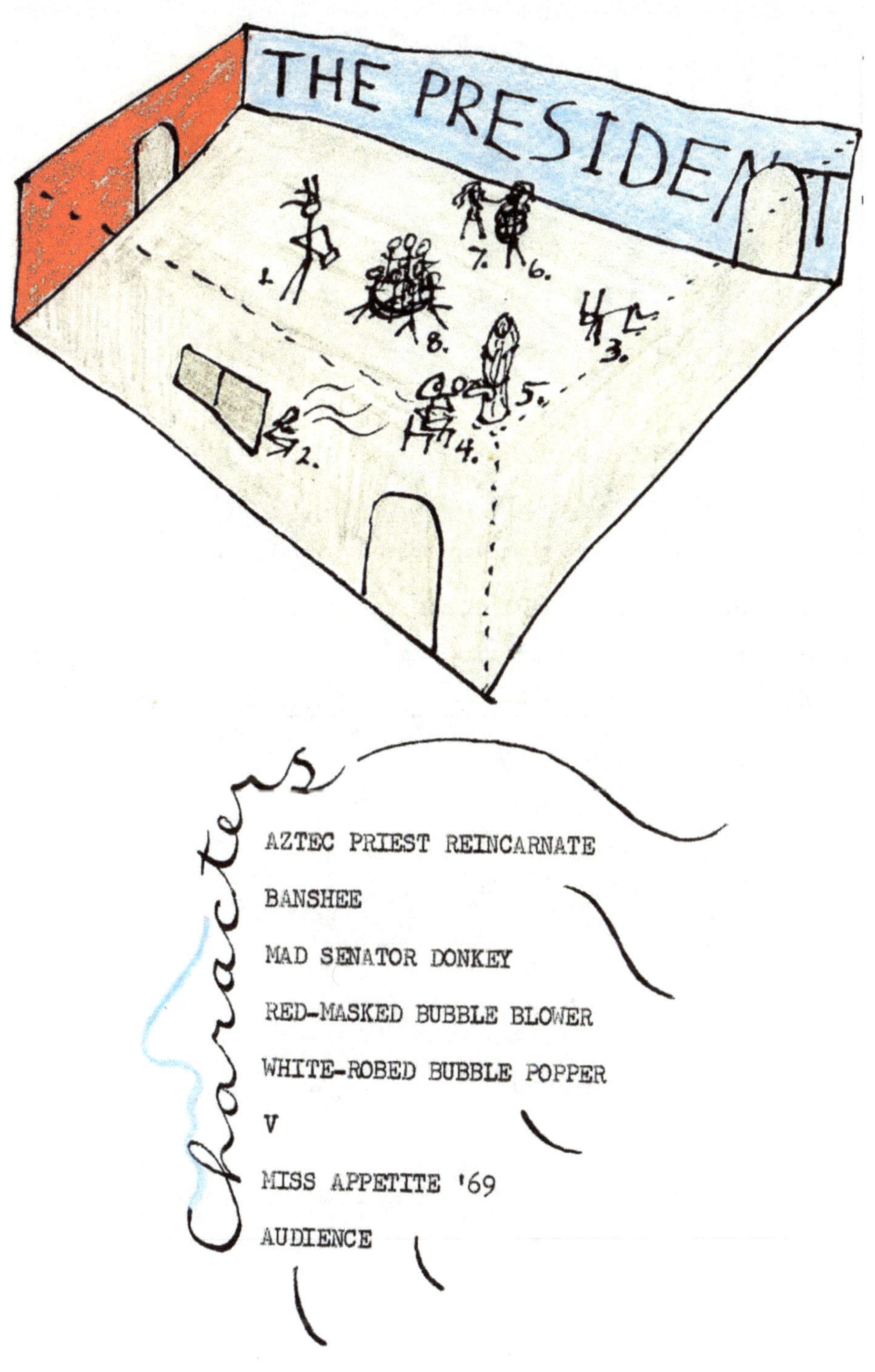

The President - event poem - wearings and shuffle cards

S H E ' S

B E E N T H E R E A L L T H E T I M E

I'm still looking at that fleck of snow

what is the gift of friends gods

that fell on my hand when Joe tossed snow in the air

or tedium or what energy to feed on

when he is the friend in this age & ever was

she could foretell the barren rocks of Eden
this paradise Placitas   growing between the rocks
a garden even into the snow

in 4 caps of acid   two women & two men
made fertile

when the entertainer of the Universe
sat on the cold shoulder   of his mirror image
& sang to us   Follow   but do not touch me
eternity is in my pants

& the age-old salt from the North
            sat in freezing temperatures
around the stove in a logging cabin
& told us the oldest story of all -- **silence**
& bushy eyebrows

underscore the maiden of Ginsberg & books
who sat in the Gemini moon & answered our questions

my question -- youve been here before many times many?

being God   on this pinnacle
a word that disappears   under my feet
go scaling thru the unfolding
Universe   arms legs extended
fingers toes just touching   the myriads you shoot thru
the only thread connected to my navel --
the entertainer's song

when paranoia beats on the door next door
the ocean flows into it   out of it
(I check at the window)

I am reluctant Adam   & Eve Gina
we stumble up the mountain garden
Lilith-Nancy   enticing   dances around us
& Joe   on the road   from a distant village
is lying back on the rocks   we are drawn to

draws   us 4   together on the bed   in this
Oriental cabaret   where all needs
are fulfilled as the Moon flows

flower out to the morning

does this all resolve?   flower out disperse
in the morning   consummation   a tiny spider
climbing his thread
          being tossed by the waves from the fire
the big cat comes in   sniffs the teapot
& lies down in intermediate sleep.

[illegible] --
          she's

been there all the time

"1968" NOTES

"Unspoken" for Michael Scrivenor, hippie "cycle-trash" (called himself) autoharpist living at my place at the time. /7
"Acid"- with Gina, Nancy, Joe, Michael (the guide). /9
"Midi" - beautiful visiting woman dancing at the Thunderbird Bar. /11
"Canniptions in Fit Meter," for Joe Bottone, living in Placitas, co-editor of *Oriental Blue Streak.* /15

Lora Linsley, Lebanese-American artist, hosting many after-reading feasts at her house in Albuquerque, cover designer for *OBS* /24
A New Land published in its entirety, pp 1-32 duende press, 2019. excerpts here are /26 & /44
"Song for Spring & The Union of Opposite Men" & "The Feast of Dreams" for Jeff Sheppard, young San Francisco poet staying at my house. /27 & 28

"4 Poems"- damp damage caused runs from dividing sheets. /34
"Circumscribed Generation" is made up of Gino August Sky, Ken Irby, Kell D. Robertson, Jr. and Ann Quin. /46
"Man Hooded." Poem minus the later title, was picked to be in *Oriental Blue Streak,* much to my now dismay. /48

"Space Orb Vision Crown" was read to bride and groom at Towapa, Las Huertas Creek, and hung in a tree by the water. /56
"She's Been There All the Time" was published in the *Placitas 69 Jelly Roll Refried Bean Bag* by Kurt Fiedler. /100

This *1968 Book* was typed and assembled, bound by 3 leather straps.

"Making it," created over night 15th of May and performed for Larry Morris's class at University of New Mexico next day, first of many presentations. /104
"The Fool" was created for Stephen Rodefer's ciass a week later - poet silently enacts history of the world while audience reads from random and prepared texts. /111
"The President" includes shuffle cards to be read, "costumes" and participants' instructions. /99

MAKING IT

poem - “a thing made”

Untie boxes, ask someone to move them around in any order and place in a straight line on the table. Open first box and read as directed, continuing on.

contents

“up till 3am then finished it in the morning, performed at Larry Morris’s two classes” University of New Mexico 15May68 and subsequently many times in classes and groups.

PROCEDURE

The 1st Magician. Don't mention title "The 1st Magician" until cards are in. Hand out little blank cards that are in the box to audience. Tell them to make up nonsense word and write it on little card. Attach red feather to hair on back of head. Pick up cards, shuffle them and announce title. Read them in somewhat declamatory way.

Ideal Poem. Contents of small box: mask, rock, necklace,
poem 1: "as simple as that rock
no more to be said
given away in the saying of it"
poem 2: "the ideal poem is one that
does not exist"

1. put on mask, 2. take out rock & look at it, 3. put on necklace & headband, 4. hold box up & take out poem #1, put box down & write #1 poem on blackboard, 5. read #1 poem. 6. take mask off, necklace off, headband off, 7. hold box up & take out poem #2, put box down, 8. write #2 on board & erase it.

Mate. 2 wooden dice, one with white dot, one with red. One word written on each side of dice.
Wooden Dice #1 (white, hold & throw from left hand)
union
orgasm
time
love
message
square
Wooden Dice #2 written on 6 sides (red, hold and throw from right hand)
magic suck go hold you below

Announce title: *Mate.* Throw and read left hand dice 4 times setting up a rhythm, throw and read right hand dice 4 times, repeat left, repeat right.

The General's Can of Mixed Nuts (or General Westmoreland's Nuts)
Put title "MIXED NUTS" on box and read "cut-up" text that's on *back of title:*
"my wife bot a can of contents labeled Mixed Nuts, peanuts, cashews, Brazil following Virginia. The picture on the can of nuts was almonds and pecans and of all of these I was depicted as a rather even mixture. But upon opening it I was amazed to find how solely of peanuts. *I* decided it seemed to consist in order to determine whether to make a count. Dec*ep*tive. The results were not the package. Cashews, 12: Brazil nuts, 3; and as follows: peanuts, 435; pecans, 2; & almonds, ½." Take out peanut from box, shell and eat it.

Poet. Shuffle cards in box and pass them out to audience and have them read one after another in order of being distributed.

The *real* Poet said, "Watch out if you quote me!"

Is this a pogum? Is that guy up there a pogut? Am *I* a pogut?

The last one to speak will set the sun back on its feet.

What do we do when we get to the end? Go around again?

"Whoever has ears to hear, let him hear."

I am next.

I know *I'm* next.

I am the tree speaking beneath these words.

Gog, id boob?

Am I next?

Is this really your favorite TV program?

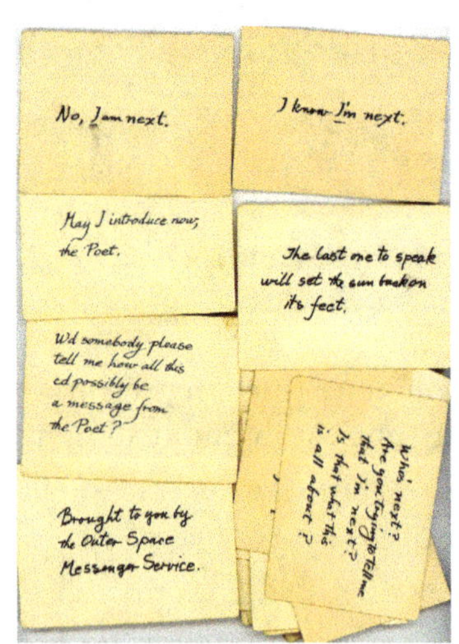

Who's next? Are you trying to tell me that I'm next? Is that what this is all about?

I'm sure I've said all this before. Why should I repeat it again?

I *know* that I can say more than is written on this card.

I think I know who the real Poet is. *She's* the real Poet.

I have a feeling that *you* are the real Poet.

The Poet said.

Would somebody please tell me how all this could possibly be a message from the Poet?

May I introduce now, the Poet.

Brought to you by the Outer Space Messenger Service.

No, *I* am next.

What if I can't read anything that's written on this card?

I keep hearing voices. Does that mean I'm qualified?

I refuse to read this card.

No.

"He who believes in himself believes in somebody else."

Are you sure you have tuned into the right frequency?

Indian. Open box fast revealing snake, unfold to become hummingbird flower poster. Display. *Ask for comments.* (Words we apply to things etc.)

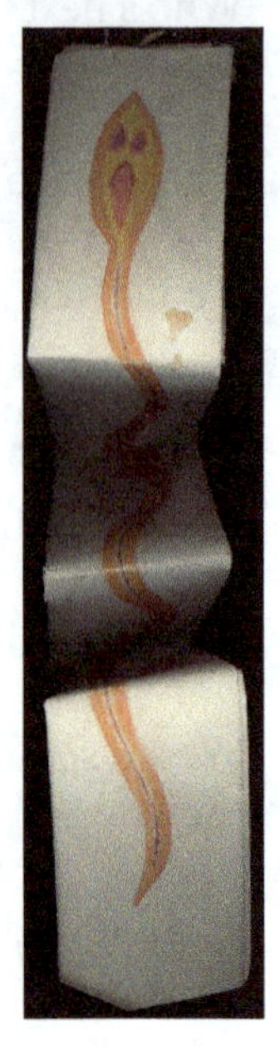

Revolution. Pass 3 by 7 inch cards out and and ask audience to write
1 something you love;
2 a verb (word of action);
3 something you hate or dislike. Display flower in box, light incense, shuffle cards and say “Revolution!” Read cards.

‘Football/ eats / German Shepherds’ -for example.
‘”Sunsets belly flop homophobia.”
“The sun pushes politics.”
“Ice cream shoots snobs.” etc.

NONSENSE WORDS CHANT

(sample) "1st Magician"
from young students - *Making It.*

21-22May68

Table also holds
Fool contents.

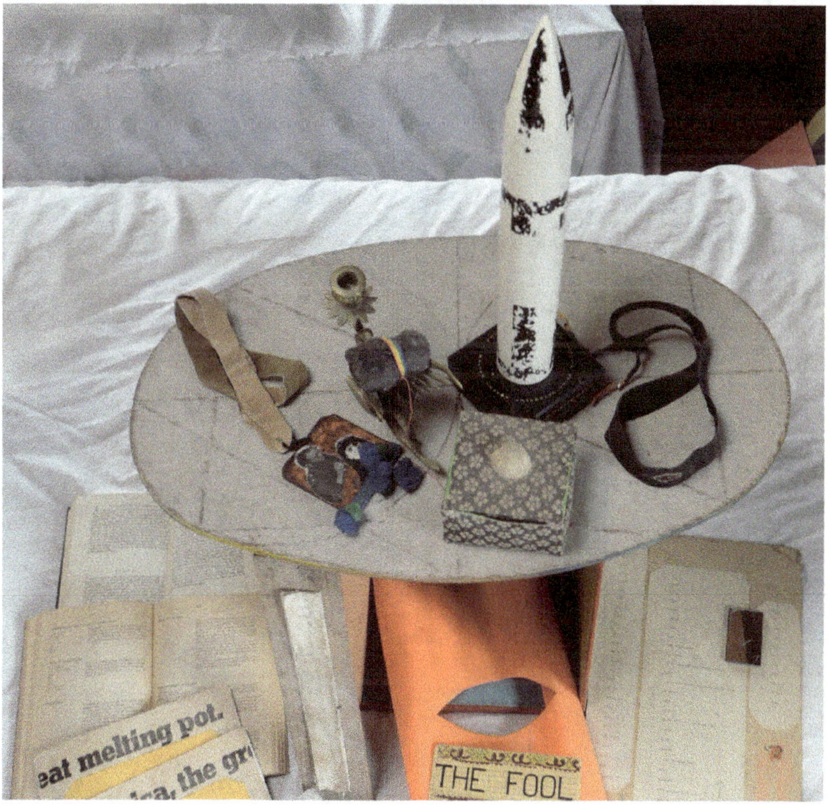

Things for *The Fool*

1 dark blue bandana
2 small box of matches ~ black & red feathers attached to it ~ picture of
a rooster on it ~ labeled The Cock
3 white candle in a winged dragon candle holder
4 wand abt 13" long ~ bird carved on the "handle" of it
5 whirler " " ~ feather attached to tip ~ 3' cord from whirler to
a small bag of seeds & spices which can be opened
6 wooden box abt 17" x 3" x 3" ~ one lengthwise side open
7 World ~ abt 6" diameter ~ made of leather, beads, thread ~ stuffed
with earth, seeds, leaves etc.
8 Moon ~ abt 2½" diameter ~ (similar to world or earth)

9 Handax ~ large enough to hold several small objects on its side ~
can be balanced on the candle holder's wings, or placed beside it

10 Necklace ~ photograph of a man & woman hang from the front of it
11 Black & White Box abt 4" x 4" x 3"
12 red feather which can be attached to the hair
13 small vial which will hold some water
14 small cup, glass, or chalice
15 small wooden jar ~ preferably shaped like a mushroom
16 some bread to go in the wooden jar

17 wooden egg ~ 3 birds painted on it

18 staff with red orange flag ~ eye shape o cut out of flag's middle

19 crown ~ flexible material (abt 20" x 14" ~ Go don in & gin bottle
visible on it (written, pictured)

20 leather strap ~ 3' long ~ used to tie the crown on around the
forehead

21 business man's tie

22 large play money dollar bill

23 model of a missile ~ abt 15" tall ~ must stand up on its
removable base ~ shd have separable booster

24 large shirt which can cover all the things on the table

25 cigaret (tobacco or herb)

26 _I Ching_, Cook Book, Egyptian _Book of the Dead_, Buddhist
Texts, etc. any of these may be used, but a cookbook
must be used

27 Poetry: 1 ~ "A, A, C, F" etc 2 ~ "same scene same scene ..."

28 table ~ abt 21" high

3 ~ "If we're left with the history of the world, what are we left with? ..."

4 ~ "In the beginning was the word, a word for turd ..."

5 ~ "sing care magic dance sing care ..."

PROCEDURE

Hand to audience items to be read. When 1st 2 finish reading (simultaneously) the next 2 read etc. Performer *(in the center)* follows the procedure & says nothing.

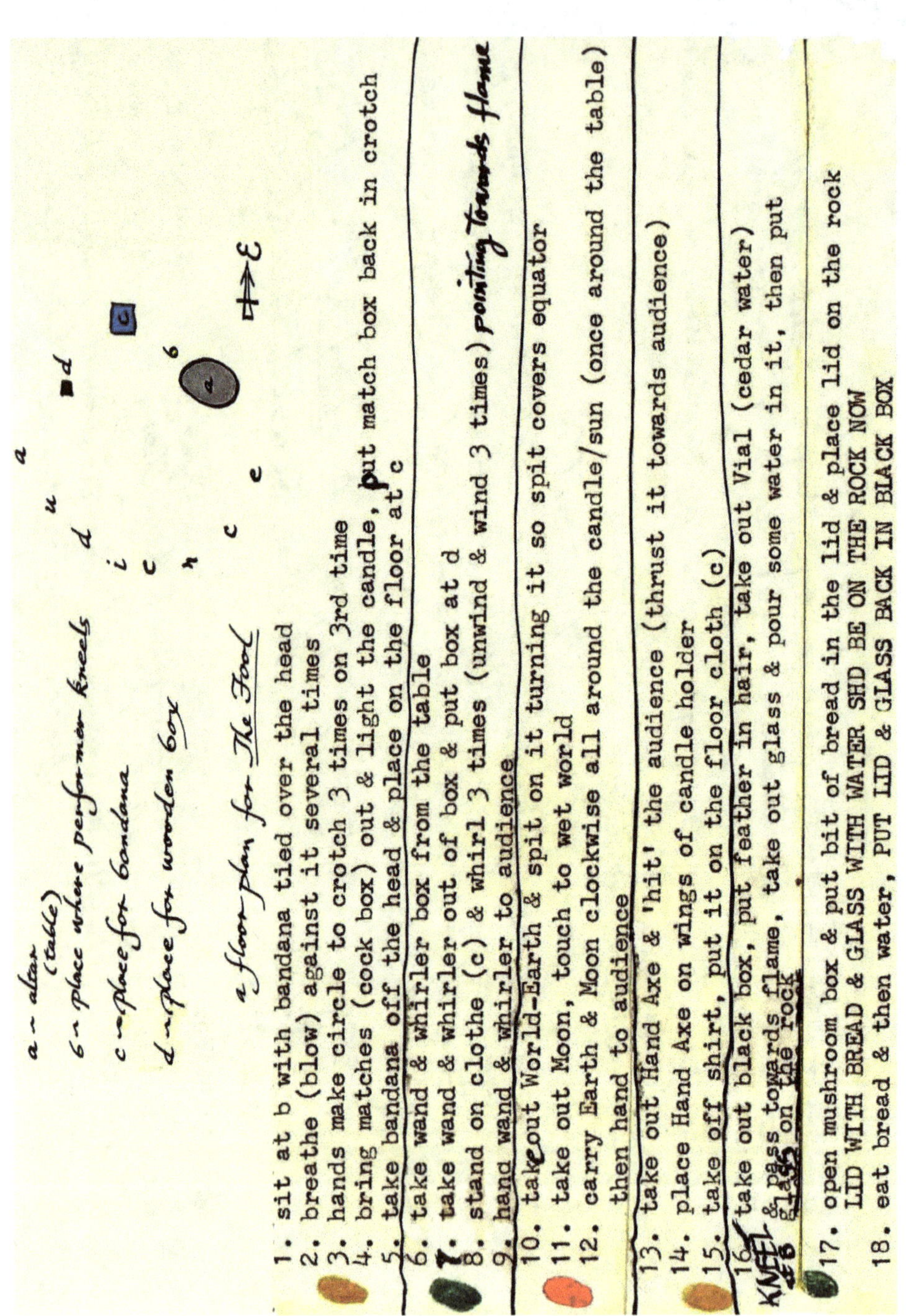
a ~ altar
(table)
b ~ place where performer kneels
c ~ place for bandana
d ~ place for wooden box

a floor plan for The Fool

1. sit at b with bandana tied over the head
2. breathe (blow) against it several times
3. hands make circle to crotch 3 times on 3rd time
4. bring matches (cock box) out & light the candle, put match box back in crotch
5. take bandana off the head & place on the floor at c
6. take wand & whirler box from the table
7. take wand & whirler out of box & put box at d
8. stand on clothe (c) & whirl 3 times (unwind & wind 3 times) pointing towards flame
9. hand wand & whirler to audience
10. take out World-Earth & spit on it turning it so spit covers equator
11. take out Moon, touch to wet world
12. carry Earth & Moon clockwise all around the candle/sun (once around the table) then hand to audience
13. take out Hand Axe & 'hit' the audience (thrust it towards audience)
14. place Hand Axe on wings of candle holder
15. take off shirt, put it on the floor cloth (c)
16. KNEEL at b take out black box, put feather in hair, take out Vial (cedar water) & pass towards flame, take out glass & pour some water in it, then put glass on the rock
17. open mushroom box & put bit of bread in the lid & place lid on the rock LID WITH BREAD & GLASS WITH WATER SHD BE ON THE ROCK NOW
18. eat bread & then water, PUT LID & GLASS BACK IN BLACK BOX

19. hold the black box up high & take the egg out, place EGG on the rock
20. take feather OUT OF THE HAIR & replace in the box
21. PUT BOX WITH STUFF IN IT ON THE BOX STAND IN FRONT (d)
22. take the necklace off, put it on the floor cloth (c) & BOW to audience
23. take the orange STAFF & bow to audience. unfurl the staff-flag, stand it against the table & PUT THE CROWN ON (tie it with the leather strap)
24. WAVE FLAG TOWARD FLAME in 8 shape (making horizontal 8 in air)
PUT IT BACK LEANING AGAINST THE TABLE
25. put tie on
26. take Dollar out & stick in back pocket
27. Kneel at b & push the shirt-cloth down exposing the MISSILE
take missile out, move it thru the air, drop its booster & zoom down
KNOCKING EGG OFF THE ROCK, give missile to the audience
28. PICK UP FLAG & WAVE IT HARD ERRATICALLY. PUTTING THE CANDLE OUT
29. put FLAG on the floor cloth (c), take DOLLAR out of pocket & put it on the floor (c). take crown off & put it & strap on floor (c)
30. 'throw' HAND AXE at the table 1& at the floor (c) & then give to the audience
31. sit down, meditate, get up & take matches from crotch & light the candle. give the match box to the audience
32. put on the table-altar-cloth-shirt. put on the necklace (it was on the floor (c)
33. get WHIRLER & whirl once at audience & open the bag at the end of the string
34. SCATTER SEEDS TO 6 DIRECTIONS then give to the audience
35. light a cigaret from the candle

SAME SCENE

Hand out column with poem on it to 2 people in audience.

same
scene
same
scene
sane
seem
sane
dream
drain
dream
sane
dream
same
seen
same
dream
drain
dream
sane
same
same
dream
drain
seem

scene
seen
scene
seen
drain
drain
same
dream
sane
scene
drain
drain
sane
scene
same
drain
dream
scene
dream
scene
dream
drain
drain
scene

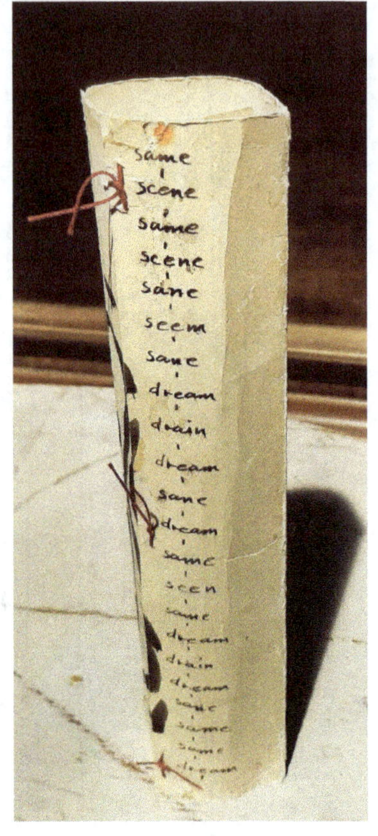

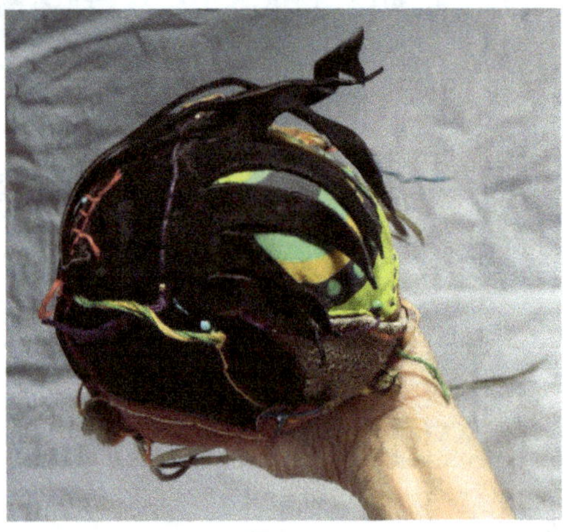

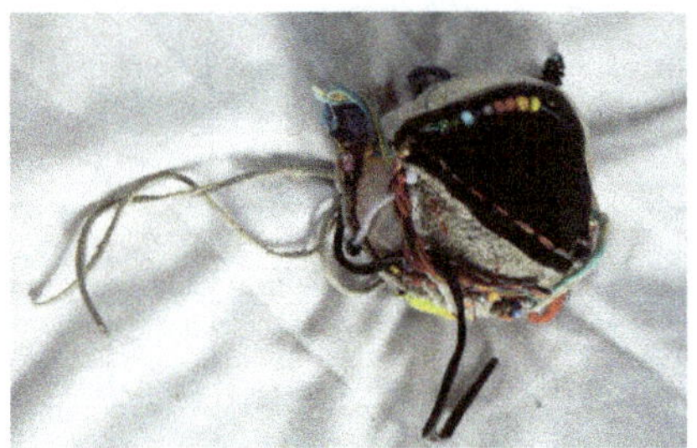

"Earth" & "Moon" used in *The Fool.*

MAKING THE "EARTH" AND THE "MOON"

"Moon" - Took many pebbles to fill the Moon. Plants. Painted much of it with white watercolor. Seeds, little ant pebbles, lichens, dirt, dead branches, an almond, abalone shell with MOON written on it, licorice root, ginger, etc.

"Earth" - Damp dirt from the sacred spring (Ojo del Horno on property), topsoil & twigs around the old grape vines, topsoil around the far out apricot tree where, tied around the trunk I found a church program – the 4 gospel writers, tore off a piece of the program and pushed it into the center of the "Earth." Dirt from the meeting of two tiny runoffs. Chamisa, apricot seeds, juniper berries, piñon needles. Dirt from around cane chollas, dirt & small pebbles from Peyote Rock – all around there, innermost recesses under the rocks, etc. Dirt from around the (huge) cottonwood tree in the arroyo. Leaves from around the prayer stones on the West side of the arroyo. Followed the arroyo up towards the old shelter cliff. Many things from the arroyo where a steep arroyo met it. Both feminine? & I masculine? Many spices – seeds – sage especially. Before closing it up.

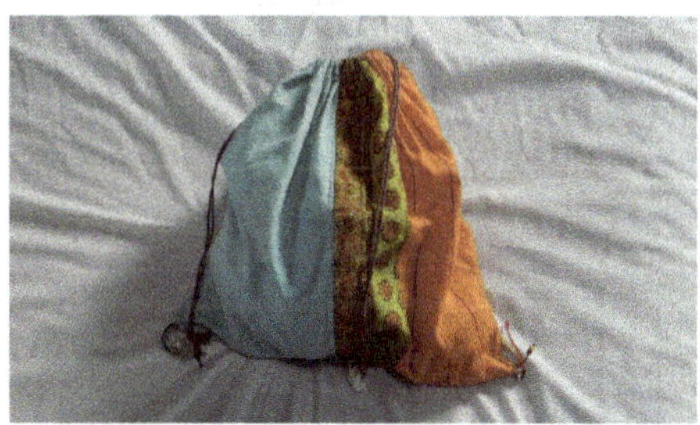

Bag for "Earth" & "Moon"

Next page is text of this "Agriculture" poem foldout to fit on 3" by 17" board.

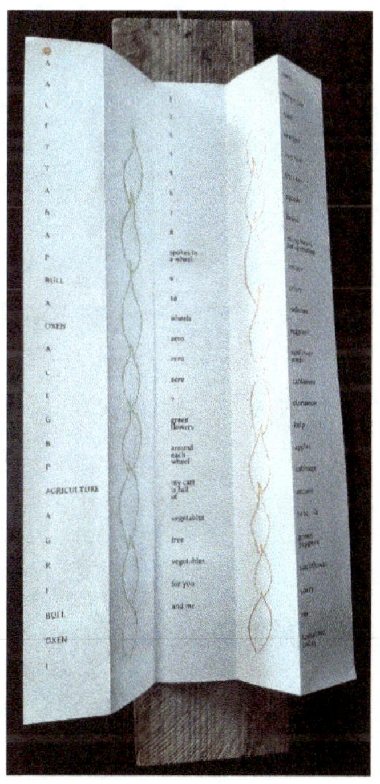

A	A	zero	beans
A	G	zero	mung beans
			for sprouting
C	R	7	
			lettuce
F	I	green	
		flowers	celery
T	BULL		
		around	radishes
T	OXEN	each	
		wheel	eggplant
A	I		
		my cart	sunflower
B	1	is full	seeds
		of	
A	2		cardamon
		vegetables	
P	3		cinnamon
		free	
BULL	4		kelp
		vegetables	
A	5		apples
		for you	
OXEN	6		cabbage
		and me	
A	7		onions
		corn	
C	8		broccoli
		brown rice	
E	spokes in		green
	a wheel	fresh	peppers
G			
	9	oranges	cauliflower
B			
	10	zucchini	sorry
P			
	wheels	fruit too	no
AGRICULTURE			
	zero	squash	tomatoes
			today.

Hand to two audience members to read.

Fool's Cap for Fool (made by Lenore Goodell)

Shuffle cards in holder
The President

Presenting "Ideal Poem" from *Making It* Bernalillo, NM

World Cook Book handed to two people to read.

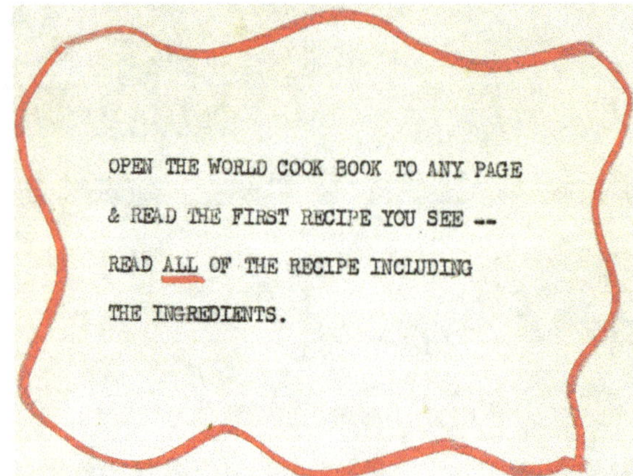

"In the Beginning" poem pasted on first page of *The Apocrypha*. Handed out to two people to read simultaneously. Next page ➜

In the beginning was the word, a word for turd.

In the beginning was a word for turd.

In the beginning was the word, a word for word.

Was it DRAT, was it DRIT, was it DRUT?   Was it insect?

In the beginning was the word, BZZZZZZZZZZZZZZZ.

In the beginning was the word, a warm word, a warm wet word.

In the beginning was the word & that word was God.

Dog   Cat   Lizard   Fish

Flower   Morning   Rainbow   Heaven

In the beginning

in the beginning

in the beginning

in the Rainbow lizard beginning was the wet morning word

in the flower heaven fish   beginning now was the word

in the insect cat beginning was the warm turd word

in the rainbow living morning   now there was a word

& the word was the beginning   & the warm God was NOW.

America, the gr

If we're left with the history of the world,

what are we left with ?

Does history pile up? Is that what we're left with?

* *(long pause)

What are we left with? Are we left with each other?

Was Joe left with Olivia?

Was Bill left with Frank?

Was June left by herself?

*

Was the shepherd left with the farmer?

Was the farmer left with the sheep?

And was there another murder?

What are we left with?

*

Were the sheep left with the Christians?

Were the Christians left with the Indians?

Were the Indians left with the psychiatrists?

Were we left here together?

*

Hand to two members of audience to read simultaneously.

eat melting pot.

Dont you remember history?   History piling up?

Which part? All of it. I remember all of it.

The whole damned history of the world.

*

If we're left with the history of the world, what are we left with ?

Not history, that's for sure. There isnt any history.

What are we left with?

Are we left with each other?

What are we left with?

outside

& in

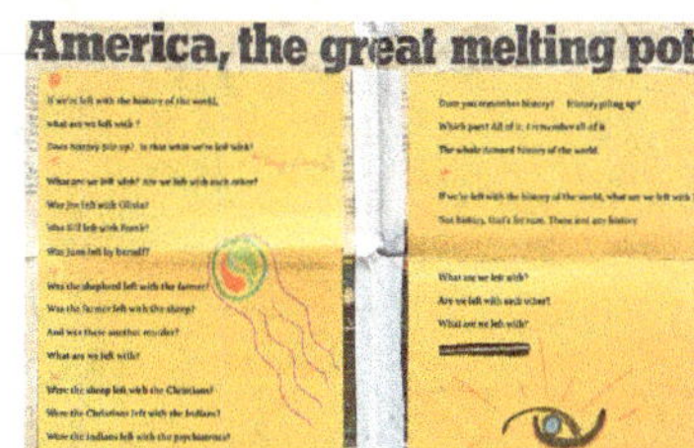

America, the great melting pot.

"Sing Care" poem with mirror-(back).

reading text➜

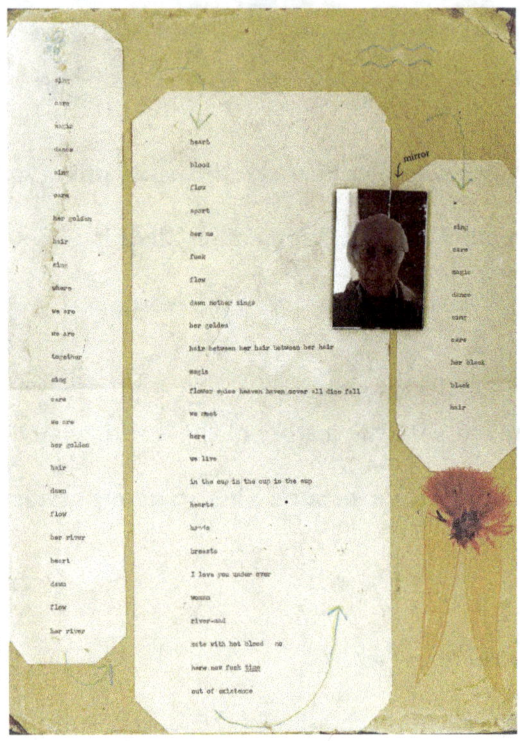

"Sing Care" (front). For 2 members of audience to read together.

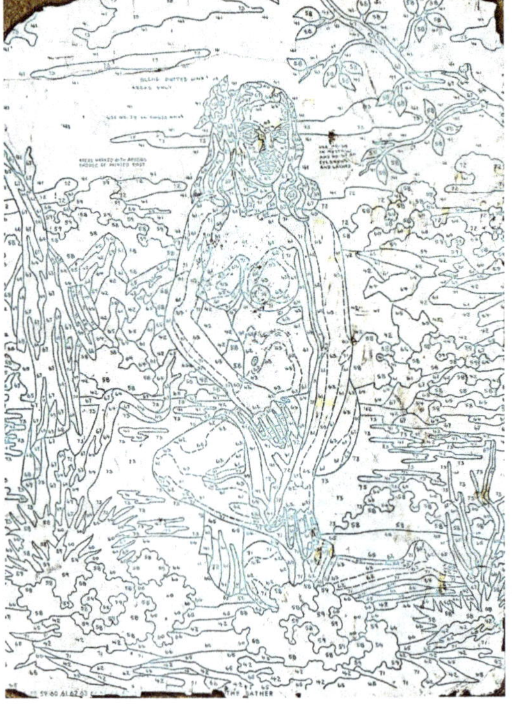

sing
care
magic
dance
sing
care
her golden
hair
sing
where
we are
we are
together
sing
care
we are
her golden
hair
dawn
flow
her river

↓
heart
blood
flow
apart
her me
fuck
flow
dawn mother sings
her golden
hair between her hair between her hair
magic
flower spice heaven haven cover all rise fall
we meet
here
we live
in the cup in the cup in the cup
hearts
hands
breasts
I love you under over
woman
river-mad
mate with hot blood   no
here now fuck time
out of existence

↓
*
sing
care
magic
dance
sing
care
her black
black
hair

"Sing Care"

SUPPLEMENT

"Cymbalation for Tray" written in February 1968 right before "Canniptions in Fit Meter" (p. 15) but not included in the *Hand Bound Book 1968*.
"Bag for the Six Directions" was from December of 1967 right after going to Zuni Shalako and preceded the "Bag" in the *Book 1968*.

CYMBALATION FOR TRAH

1.

a martha pew
& that was all the binges "A"

a card a wonka
tōnt?
lips
yrs
– marks on the page→
like a cloud
my hand was in dishes

wa
ter.

2.

peril
& toss
no go
hymn→
chant

Tarnst

a fish
will swim

oh
Joe

3.

a *laugh-*
& pear
all that rain?
power

nugget
in yr groin

away
from there

4.

I pi̲ll it
bing
tange & way
yo̲u grow?
tōmay?

a flower on the mountain dough

5.

Harry→
ston
February

all toe blow down
around-
lu-
tion

Chōgosinay?

we̲
not

6.

She
Chri̱st
tele
phone hallst
& back
& you
i̱n spring
& verge

terraced for growing grown
love har

7.

in ancient times
south acres twice
we
go

there-
is
not
kite in the

sun is
two-
bag

for us & hers there too

BAG FOR THE 6 DIRECTIONS

Cards contained in clear plastic bag and attached to door of the room, with title showing, Alternative title: SACRIFICE. Written *late '67* after Ann Quin and I went to Shalako ceremonies at Zuni Pueblo.

colors from Notebook #7 - Apr-Dec 68

1968 for me was a downright remarkable year. I was 33. I was in a play we called **Wherever She Blows** in which Bill and Meredith Pearlman and Mel Buffington and a dancer named Gandalf and I made the whole thing up. Bill and Mel and I ended the thing by each of us reading a poem when the spotlight would hit, and I did things to the back of my poems. I became aware of the backs of all my poems. I fixed them up and did designs on them. I would tear a poem in two when I was reading it in the spotlight. We slowly as the spotlight went from one to the other began to move away from page dependency and would make up poems. Make up things, jump up and down.

Later in the Spring that year Larry Morris asked me to talk to his class at UNM. I was up all night putting together magic box poems called **Making It**, which is the meaning of poetry. In each of the seven different boxes there was a different event poem, all the way from word sounds to chance, from cut-up method to semantic punning, the audience writing the poems for two of the boxes. (I handed IBM cards out and had them write things on them and then shuffled them and read them.) One called **General Westmoreland's Nuts** had peanuts in it which I ate as I read a Burroughs cut-up of a mixed nuts can label. One called **Ideal Poem** had the first useful mask I've ever made in it, a little collapsible silvery thing that fit over my eyes. Somebody would mix all the boxes around and I would go through them one by one.

I did this for Larry Morris's class and a week later I went into Steve Rodefer's class after having stayed up all night putting together a thing called **The Fool**. In this event poem I read **nothing at all.** I handed to the audience cardboard, paper and a tube with poems on them, and I handed them the **I Ching**, the **World Cook Book**, the Egyptian **Book of the Dead**, say, etc. and they went around in a circle two people reading simultaneously, reading the page they'd happened to open the book up to, or the poem I'd handed them. While this chanting went on I was busy at my Magician's table going through the motions of creating the world. I'd made replicas of the Earth and the Moon and many more things. And I kept moving around never saying a word but following my ritual directives step by step. At one point I had a huge Texas dollar bill sticking out of my hip pocket, a huge Gordon's Gin headdress, a tie on but no shirt on, and I'm moving a plastic replica of the Polaris missile through the air. I screw everything up and have to start creating the world all over again. I scatter seeds from a pouch that's tied to the end of my world-creating whirler and sit down, and that's the end of **The Fool.**

Now that I look back on it I was getting as far away as possible from a typical monologue poetry reading which I'd been to hundreds of times by then. I do not feel that an audience has **any** obligation to listen to a poet read his or her work. If it's boring just get up and leave.

I am dedicated entirely to oral poetry. Reading is a nice thing to do especially to discover secondary sources which might ignite the primary source which is yourself. For contemporary poetry, hearing it from the poet is the test, no matter what the lit critters say. Increasingly you can give space to someone's voice, but your life can get jammed up with the printed word. So all the more important for that voice to be worth hearing. [Charles] Olson told us young poets we weren't doing things large enough, we had little bits-and-pieces poems. That big man told us that and struck a reverberant chord in me. I've always been interested in risking myself at the boundaries others impose on me. I've always wanted large forms. Novels, plays, events, creating a world—but never just the single poem with somebody's explication on the opposite page. The job of the poet is "to build us his world," Ezra Pound said.

Now that I look back on it I was exploring to the hilt the tremendous longing for rite in me. Living all my life in New Mexico observing people with their own meaningful rituals, I wanted my own, and had only me to come up with it. **The Fool** allowed me to be a Magician and at the same time realize who exactly I am, a Scotch-Irish-Cur-New Mexican, skinny and with too high a voice. And whenever things got too serious there I was the FOOL. Magician and Fool at once. The sacred and the profane. The clown-priest, but not really, just me. The **I Ching** and the Tarot figure constantly in my notebooks at this time. Taking of sorts. Pointing the finger at a text and reading. Shuffling cards and reading. And writing poems.

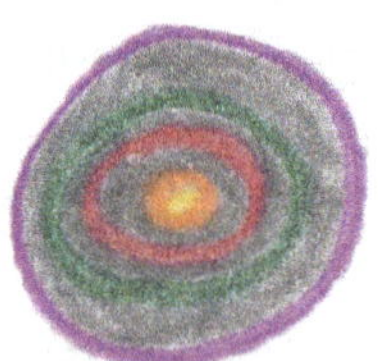

A CULMINATION OF 1968

Lenore Schwartz, a New York sculptor and photographer, received her MA from the University of New Mexico and we met. She and I went to Mexico City and visited Coatlicue, Aztec Cosmos-Earth-Goddess, in the National Museum of Anthropology. On December 2ND we got married in Placitas, and drove to NYC to see art and visit her family. When we got back it seemed a most worthy and lasting end to the year, and we settled down to our high Placitas garden.

Larry Goodell

END

1968

bound & related poems

from notebook April '68

BY THE AUTHOR

Dance Book (poetry and dance collaborations) 2023.
Between Ann and Larry - 1965 to 1973 - duende press 2023.

Escape - poems 2003-2007; Grounded - poems 2008-2010.
Commons - poems 2017-2019 duende press 2020.

Nothing To Laugh About - poems 2015-2016 Beatlick Press 2018.
Pieces of Heart - poems of 2014 Beatlick Press 2018.
Digital Remains - poems of 2013 Beatlick Press 2018.
Broken Garden & The Unsaid Sings - poems 2011 & 2012 Beatlick Press 2015.

Hot Art & Other Plays - (collected plays) duende press 2019.
A New Land & Other Writings - (collected prose) duende press 2019.

Here On Earth - 59 Sonnets La Alameda Press 1996.

Out of Secrecy - poems by Larry Goodell Yoo-Hoo Press 1992.
Firecracker Soup - poems 1980-1987 Cinco Puntos Press 1990.

Seven Sonnets - duende press 1987.
The Mad New Mexican - (Songs 1981-86) Ubik Sound 1986.
Dawn Ladder - San Marcos Press 1981?

Sunlove Gypsy - (mimeo) duende press 1967.
Cycles - author's first book, edited and with a foreword by William
(Latif) Harris, (mimeo) duende press 1966.

Website, blogs http://www.larrygoodell.com/
Spoken word archives & improvised music
https://duende.bandcamp.com/
Videos https://www.youtube.eom/@larrygoodell66
larrynewmex@gmail.com

"One must not come to feel that he has
a thousand threads in his hands,
He must somehow see the one thing;
This is the level of art
There are other levels
But there is no other level of art."

- George Oppen (1908-1984)

www.ingramcontent.com/pod-product-compliance
Lightning Source LLC
LaVergne TN
LVHW050537100826
845148LV00002B/594

9780915008193